CONGRESSIONAL
COMMITTEES

Jill Duvall

Democracy in Action

FRANKLIN WATTS
A Division of Grolier Publishing
New York London Hong Kong Sydney
Danbury, Connecticut

Photographs ©: AP/Wide World Photos: 50, 51, 83; Corbis-Bettmann: 11, 28, 35, 76; Folio, Inc.: cover (Ashe), 58 (William Bradstreet), 45 (Rob Crandall), 56 (Drew Harmon), 70, 96 (David Marie), 91 (Michael Patrick); Gamma-Liaison: 86 (Cynthia Johnson); Jay Mallin: 14, 42, 47, 65, 80, 95; Time/Life Pictures: 20 (William Bradstreet).

Library of Congress Cataloging-in-Publication Data

Duvall, Jill.
Congressional committees / Jill Duvall
        p. cm. — (Democracy in action)
        Includes bibliographical references and index.
        Summary: Examines the different types of committees in Congress, their functions, leadership, and influences.
        ISBN: 0-531-11343-4
        1. United States. Congress—Committees—Juvenile literature. [1. United States. Congress—Committees.] I. Title. II. Series: Democracy in action (Franklin Watts, inc.)
        JK1029.D88 1997
        328.73'0765—dc21   96-48495
                                                                        CIP
                                                                        AC

CONTENTS

INTRODUCTION

In a democracy, perhaps the most important
duty of the government is to make the people's
will into public policy by means of law. The
importance of this can be seen by the fact that the
first and longest Article of the Constitution deals
with the legislative branch.
— DREWRY AND O'CONNOR, *America Is* (1995)

The Congress of the United States is one of the most fascinating institutions ever devised—and easily one of the most puzzling. Countless diagrams have been designed, with boxes and arrows pointing in all directions, trying to explain our national legislature. These diagrams show only part of the story, at best.

The U.S. Constitution provides details about who can serve in the national legislative branch and establishes the duties of those lawmakers. What the Constitution doesn't say is how the Founding Fathers expected Congress to actually *do* its work. Thus, since its first meeting in 1789, the legislative body has had to invent itself. That same year saw the creation of the first Congressional committee.

Article I of the Constitution establishes that there must be two houses of Congress but gives little instruction about their internal organization. It does not mention committees at all. Nonetheless, most of the work of Congress is done in committees. "The daily routines . . . [and] indeed the careers of nearly all members are structured by committee duties."[1]

Each chamber has developed a distinct structure, and each makes its own rules. Both the House of Representatives and the Senate have many committees. The House even has a committee appointed by the Clerk of the House of Representatives for the sole purpose of escorting the newly elected Speaker to his chair.[2] The "mechanics" of the committee system can be readily depicted, but pictures cannot fully explain the way committees function. One reason is the four major political groups involved: Senate Democrats, Senate Republicans, House Republicans, and House Democrats. Despite party labels, each member is free to vote from conscience or constituent preference, even if that decision differs from party leadership.

Further adding to the confusion is the variety of committees. The number of committees and their names are not identical in the two chambers, and not all committees are created with the same levels of influence. In the House, for example, the Rules Committee, "which specifies the conditions under which all bills are debated and amended," is extraordinarily powerful.[3] There is no committee like the House Rules Committee in the Senate. Rules governing committee behavior also are different in the separate chambers.

Up until the 1970s, the position of committee chairperson was a very powerful one. When the rules were changed in 1974, the subcommittee chairperson obtained a greater share of power. This distribution of power, especially in the House, was expected to give voters more confidence in the Congress. Abuse of power has been one of the main reasons for periodic attempts to pass reform measures. Unfortunately, the public is still all too frequently treated to reports of unethical or illegal behavior involving elected legislators. It is difficult to trust members of Congress to resolve society's problems while they are busy defending their own behavior.

One of the most significant problems in comprehending the Congressional committee system is the difficulty in observing the exercise of power, both institutional and personal. Institutional power comes to members through the duties assigned them by the Constitution. Money bills and impeachment resolutions, for example, must originate in the House. The

Senate alone confirms presidential appointees and ratifies treaties. These duties are unchangeable.

On the other hand, personal power is not so easily measured. Such issues as which members are powerful, how they use or abuse power, and how they maintain their power are anything but stable. A great deal of this power is exercised within the confines of committees.

Within the two chambers, power is divided among minority and majority party members, among leaders who have accumulated personal power, and among the old guard and the new. These powers are in constant flux and are subject to a variety of changes: international events, such as wars or natural disasters; unfavorable or more favorable economic conditions in the United States; changes in the traditions and norms in House or Senate chambers; and inevitable reverses in public opinion.

For example, Representative Newt Gingrich (R-Georgia)* became the Speaker of the House at the beginning of the 104th Congress. The House had just obtained a majority of Republicans; 73 of them were newly elected. Gingrich and many of the so-called freshmen had committed themselves to a campaign pledge called the Contract with America. The new Congressional members assumed that this commitment to certain reforms of the federal government was extremely important to American voters. They believed the Contract had been instrumental in giving the Republicans a majority in the House, which had for 40 years had a majority of Democrats.

Speaker Gingrich's popularity was very high at the beginning of the two-year Congressional session. After two shutdowns of the federal government and the passage of only a smattering of the legislation called for in the Contract, the Speaker's popularity dropped severely. Yet, at the beginning of the second half of the session, he was still the same man—in the same job. Voter opinion had changed. It will not be clear for

---

*Information in parentheses identifies the political party and home state of members of Congress.

some time whether Gingrich regains all the personal power he had at the beginning of the 104th Congress.

Traditions and norms change, too. Seniority in selection of committee chairpersons and an unwritten rule that freshmen are expected to be silent until they learn how Congress works are no longer strictly followed. Civility, which has been a tradition in the Senate for two centuries, may be on the endangered list.[4] Some incumbents who have chosen not to run for reelection have given this change in manners as a prominent reason for their decision. Not since the very earliest Congresses, when members were not professional politicians, have there been so many voluntary retirements. Early retirements, deaths, and indictments each claim a share of members. Although these changes might seem insignificant in a body of more than five hundred officeholders, the departure of a sizable number of members has an impact on the Congress.

Understanding how committees in Congress work requires a basic knowledge of the types and functions of those units. Knowing how party leaders are chosen and recognizing the many outside influences felt by members will help to explain aspects of committee behavior. Raising and spending the nation's money and keeping careful watch over the agencies created to carry out these processes are two essential responsibilities of the Congress. We'll explore these topics to gain a greater understanding of the operations of congressional committees.

Chapter 1

TYPES OF COMMITTEES

We can set up permanent processes.
We may not be able to set up
permanent decisions.

—WOODROW WILSON, 1919

At present, there are about 250 Congressional committees and subcommittees. Within recent two-year cycles, 100 senators and 435 representatives have had to deal with more than 10,000 bills, a federal budget exceeding $1.5 trillion, thousands of constituent problems, and hundreds of federal appointments requiring confirmation.[1] For most members, these tasks were in addition to other activities, including running for reelection. Maintaining a Congressional seat has become almost a full-time occupation for many members.

Although "lawmaker" is the best-known job description of a member of Congress, an equally important function is that of public educator. Through hearings and interactions with constituents and the media, national issues receive public exposure. Although many proposals now originate in the executive branch, only members of Congress can introduce bills into the legislature and transform those bills into law. The standing rules of each chamber assign several different powers to committees. Some can create legislation, and most are able report bills to the full membership of their chamber. All committees can gather information but not every one is authorized to write or report legislation.[2]

Committee names can be mystifying: select, standing, special, conference, joint, ad hoc—to name just a few. There are also campaign committees, steering and policy committees, task forces, and advisory commissions, all of which function as parts of the internal structure of Congress. The most significant distinctions among these units are their tenure and legislative or reporting authority.

STANDING COMMITTEES

Standing committees and most of their subcommittees are permanent, have permanent staffs, and have legislative authority. "The standing committees of Congress, operating as little legislatures, determine the fate of most legislative proposals."[3] A committee has several options once a bill has been referred to it for consideration. If the committee does not reject the measure immediately, it frequently calls for hearings. Also, the committee staff can rewrite the bill before any other action is taken. Then the committee can approve the measure and send it to the parent chamber. A bill that the committee does not favor can also be sent to the chamber, thus giving to the full membership the responsibility of dealing with the proposal. A bill rejected by a committee generally is said to have died in committee. Any bill sent to the floor of the Senate or House is said to have been reported out.

AD HOC, SPECIAL, AND SELECT COMMITTEES

Most ad hoc, joint, select, special committees, task forces, and commissions are not permanent and do not have legislative authority. Ordinarily, such committees have been established to conduct specific investigations—for example, the Select Committee on Presidential Campaign Activities (also known as the Watergate Committee).

In July 1973, Senator Sam Ervin (far right) speaks with other members of the Select Committee on Presidential Campaign Activities. The Senate Watergate Committee, as the it is better known, is one example of a select committee, which is a temporary committee that does not have legislative authority.

The two Select Intelligence committees, one in each chamber, are the exception to this rule. Despite their official titles, these two committees are permanent because no time limit was set on their existence when they were established. They function just as other standing committees do and have legislative and budgeting authority over the Central Intelligence Agency, Defense Intelligence Agency, National Security Council, and some aspects of the Federal Bureau of Investigation.[4]

JOINT COMMITTEES

Joint committees are usually created for housekeeping or investigative purposes. As their name implies, they involve members of both chambers. Joint committees generally are permanent committees but lack authority to report legislation. At present, there are four joint committees. These committees have been created for a wide variety of reasons, including making recommendations for reforms.

The Joint Committee on Printing handles matters relating to Congressional documents, most of which are prepared by the Government Printing Office. Although no budget was provided for the Joint Committee on the Library of Congress for the 104th Congress, the committee still exists. Members of the committee decided its functions were worth keeping. As with all joint committees, the title of chairperson rotates from Senate to House at the beginning of each two-year cycle. The chairpeople have provided staff from their own offices to convene meetings and conduct business concerning the Library of Congress. The two other joint committees, the Joint Committee on Taxation and the Joint Economic Committee, assist other committees in setting national policy, especially in the budgeting process.

CAMPAIGN COMMITTEES

On the first day of each new Congress, Democrats and Republicans are well aware that they will soon start their next reelection campaigns. To help them in that endless endeavor, they select individuals from their party to serve on campaign committees. These committees have no policy-making authority and are not even connected to the national party campaign committees. In fact, they do not involve themselves in the primaries or platforms for the party conventions.

Using volunteer funds, the campaign committees maintain offices in the District of Columbia and concentrate primarily on the reelection of members. Service on one of the campaign committees is one of the ways members amass power and advance in the House or Senate hierarchy. In addition to raising funds for individual incumbents, these committees provide research on issues, develop voter turn-out strategies, and organize volunteer support in home districts.

Despite evidence that the public wants serious campaign finance reform, members of Congress seem bent on ignoring the problem. On June 25, 1996, the Senate voted once again to kill "the 25-year drive to curb spending and special-interest influence on House and Senate elections."[4] It is not difficult to understand public cynicism when the president and the Speaker of the House, in a widely publicized event in June 1995, had pledged to study ways to reform campaign financing.

CONFERENCE COMMITTEES

Conference committees are a form of joint committee, and they have a very explicit function. They exist only so long as they are needed to reconcile the differences between House and Senate bills. Only when House and Senate bills are identical are they sent to the president to be signed into law or vetoed. Each chamber has created standing rules that govern much of conference committee structure. Rules outline responsibilities, establish procedures, and (in the Senate) even determine the size of committees.[5] This special form of committee will be discussed in chapter 2.

HOUSE RULES COMMITTEE

Every major piece of legislation being considered by committees in the House of Representatives must go to the Rules Committee. This committee sets the conditions under which debate and amendments are to be handled when a bill or resolution is being considered by the full membership. The Rules Committee can limit time for discussion and bar all amendments.[7] It even has the power to block a bill from being considered on the floor.

In 1996, a House-Senate conference committee works to reconcile House and Senate versions of a welfare reform bill.

When hearings are conducted, only the members of a committee requesting a rule appear to testify. The House Parliamentarian then drafts the rules into a resolution that must be voted upon by the whole chamber. According to George B. Galloway, whose *History of the House of Representatives* (1976) was the first comprehensive study of that institution, this committee serves as the majority leadership's main method for controlling the business of the House.

COMMITTEE OF THE WHOLE

By constantly having to invent itself, Congress has created unique ways of carrying out its tasks. One of its methods is the process called Committee of the Whole House. This technique temporarily amends the House rules so that 100 members constitute a quorum, instead of the 218 members necessary for a simple majority. The procedure begins when the Speaker designates a party colleague to preside over the "committee" for the purpose of general debate.

Sponsors of measures are given five minutes to defend their positions. Opponents also receive five minutes. A vote could then be taken, but as can be imagined, members have figured several ways to avoid ending the debate. Overall, though, things move along more rapidly because a smaller quorum is required. The Senate, with a membership less than one-quarter of that of the House, does not consider legislation in a Committee of the Whole. On the House side, "in practice, most important bills are considered in Committee of the Whole."[8]

Members need only glance at the Speaker's platform to see if the House is in regular session. If it is, a mace (an ornamental staff) will have been placed on the green marble pedestal to the right of the Speaker's chair. If the Sergeant of Arms has moved the mace to the lower white marble pedestal, the House is functioning as a Committee of the Whole.

HOW THE COMMITTEES WORK

Just as in other matters in the House or Senate, members present a resolution in the appropriate chamber to create a committee. The full membership votes on the measure. Size, duration, and jurisdiction of the committee are usually included in the written resolution that creates it. At the end of each two-year session, all committees officially expire. On opening day of the next session, the standing committees are voted on in a simple procedure instead of being re-created through new resolutions. All others are automatically dissolved unless action to reconstitute them is taken.

At the beginning of the 105th Congress in January 1997, there were 19 standing committees in the House and 16 in the Senate. Any committee having 15 or more members is required to have at least four subcommittees. Subcommittees are smaller units of the full committee and have specific jurisdictions. In this way, committee work can be reasonably divided. It would be virtually impossible for lawmakers to sort out complicated legislation in most of the full committees, which can have large numbers of participants.

Most diagrams of how federal laws are made include one box labeled "the hopper." There actually is a box in each chamber into which a member can place an unlimited number of proposals for new legislation. More frequently, however, the documents are handed to the clerk of the chamber. Members do not have to seek recognition from the presiding officer in order to introduce a bill in this manner.

Senate and House Offices of Legislative Counsel have been created to assist lawmakers in drafting legislation. These offices are staffed with lawyers who are experienced at turning proposals into appropriate legal wording, a skill individual Congressional members do not always possess.

The measure now begins a journey that lasts until it is enrolled and returns to the House or Senate floor for a final vote or until the end of the Congressional session. If the bill is stuck somewhere along the way and not passed by the end of the session, it is not carried forward to the next session. The process must be started anew if members wish to continue trying to pass the measure. One exception to this practice is treaties. They do not expire at the end of a legislative session but continue their journey through the Senate's ratification process.

Bills are labeled with sponsors' names (any number of sponsors), referred to committees, and finally sent to the Government Printing Office. Standing rules (initially House Rule X and Senate Rule XXV) detail the procedures for referral, that is, determine which committee will consider a particular piece of proposed legislation.

$\mathcal{T}$HE PARLIAMENTARIANS

The Parliamentarian's function is little discussed, but it is important and perhaps one of the most unusual in the Congress. Each house has its own parliamentarian, who has a personal staff. The House Parliamentarian acts on behalf of the Speaker, the Senate Parliamentarian on that of the presiding officer. When a referral is made, the procedure is called the first reading although the bill is not actually read on the floor at that time.[9]

The Speaker appoints the parliamentarian in the House, "without regard to political affiliation and solely on the basis of fitness to perform the duties of the position."[10] Additional duties include advising the committee chairpersons on procedures at any time the House is in session. Confidential consultations on legislative and parliamentary matters are available to all members of Congress. Agencies of the government consult with the Office of the Parliamentarian on a regular basis, and the office is in charge of arranging programs for House ceremonies, such as joint sessions. This office carries out one of the constitutionally mandated functions, that of preparing an official record of the House, called the Journal. Two centuries of Congressional activity have added greatly to the complex position of parliamentarian, without whom chaos would reign.

According to the *Congress Dictionary*, the parliamentarian is "always on the floor and constantly murmuring advice . . . [and] is a virtual ventriloquist, sometimes whispering one sentence at a time so the presiding officer gets it right." Also, according to the *Dictionary*, "The Parliamentarian and his staff are experts in ways to route legislation to the most appropriate—and most sympathetic—committees, for finding precedents for rulings, and for setting strategy for floor debates."[11]

Chapter **2**

COMMITTEE
FUNCTIONS

When we deliberate, it is about means, not ends.
—ARISTOTLE, *Nicomachean Ethics*

Now that we've identified the types of committees and gained a general sense of their structure, let's take a look at the inner workings of committees.

MULTIPLE REFERRALS

After their introduction in their parent chamber, most bills are referred to a single committee for consideration. Because committee jurisdictions often overlap, the practice of multiple referral, or sending a bill to more than one committee, is being used more and more frequently. "Committees guard their jurisdictional turfs closely, and the parliamentarians know and follow the precedents."[1]

There are three types of multiple referral: joint, sequential, and split. With joint referrals, an entire bill is assigned to two or more committees or subcommittees for simultaneous consideration. Sequential referral means an entire bill is assigned to one committee at a time, with a schedule for each unit to complete its work before sending it to the next one. Split referrals divide bills into pieces and refer sections to the most appropriate committees or subcommittees. The individual pieces are considered at the same time within the different committees. "Most multiple referrals involve just two committees, although cases involving more than two committees are not uncommon. Indeed, the total number has been as great as fifteen."[2]

Using memoranda of intent, committees of the Senate often prepare referral agreements before bills are assigned, thus avoiding most turf disputes. There is seldom a need to challenge the parliamentarian's decisions.

In the House, joint referral was ended at the beginning of the 104th Congress, but sequential and split referrals are still used. Increasingly, task forces are used to assist in preparing legislation.[3] When a bill concerns a particularly sensitive issue, the many participants involved within the legislative process work out strategies for passing legislation. These strategies can become extremely complex. Maneuvering for "friendly" bill referrals has become a standard part of the process.

HEARINGS AND WRITTEN COMMENTS

During consideration of bills, members and staff obtain information from various sources, including government agencies, interest groups, experts, and the public. Government officials are asked either to appear in person or to send written comments to the committee. The public and other interested parties also submit testimony and other types of information to help the committee determine the potential impact of the proposed legislation.

Timely notices of hearings are published in the *Congressional Record*, including the names of expected witnesses and summaries of the agenda. Hearings are not trials but are considered valuable information-gathering sessions, allowing all sides to be heard before the full Congress votes on the legislation. On docket days, authors of bills are invited to brief staff and members on the contents and to discuss why they believe the legislation is necessary.

Testifiers need not be sworn in. "Under Senate rules, most

In 1995, a House committee holds Medicare hearings outside the Capitol Building. During consideration of bills, committees hold hearings to get information from various sources, including the public.

committees require one senator to be present when sworn testimony is taken; otherwise any remarks made are interviews with no legal weight. When a special committee is created, however, the Senate often votes to give committee staff the authority to take sworn testimony with a senator present."[4] In the House, most hearings are held by subcommittees, but any member of the full committee can attend and question witnesses.[5] The public is invited to attend the majority of hearings. To facilitate this, hearings are not restricted to Washington, D.C., but are held throughout the nation. Special care is taken to ensure that congressional members in regions likely to be affected by proposed laws will be able to question knowledgeable witnesses from the area. Some hearings involve decisions that have an impact on other areas of the world, as discussed in chapter 7.

According to Walter J. Oleszek, one of the most knowledgeable scholars of Congressional procedures, "Hearings are perhaps the most orchestrated phase of policy making and are part of any overall strategy to get bills enacted into law. Committee members and staff typically plan with care who should testify, when, and on what issues."[6]

ARKUP

Formal meetings of subcommittees and committees are most often held for *markup*, the process used for working out amendments, incorporating information submitted during the hearings phase, and determining the language to be used in the final bill. Normally, each section of the bill is taken up separately. If amendments are made, that section is voted on before the next one is considered. Finally, the entire bill is voted upon by the members.[7] The final stage of the markup process is the preparation of detailed reports for the full committee or full chamber.

Most members of the Senate consider subcommittee markups a waste of time. The most efficient use of subcommittee efforts, they believe, is conducting hearings. Therefore, the Senate has a two-stage system: subcommittees do the basic research, and full committees do markups.[8]

Only on very rare occasions will there be no changes in the original bill. It is also rare for a committee to send a bill to the parent chamber with a recommendation that it not be approved. It is much easier to simply ignore the bill. If the decision is to go forward, the chairperson is responsible for seeing that the results are reported out.

Committee reports often have lengthy analyses of amendments, minority reports, tables, charts, and other materials. Included are notices of changes to existing laws and costs or other impacts that these changes are likely to have.

Records of committee voting are kept and made available to the public. The reports are not easy to follow, but the original bill can be examined, as well as the amended one, with strike-throughs and italics to indicate the changes made in the final bill.

Full copies of committee reports are made available to all members prior to any further activity on the bill. Committees only make recommendations; the fate of the bill is in the hands of the entire Congress and the president.

HOLDS

Only the Senate uses *holds*. One or more senators (their names are not divulged) can make a request to party leaders that certain measures not be allowed out of committee or not be brought to the floor in any other way. That is all that is required for silencing of the issue in the Senate chamber.

There is no way to know who has placed a hold, how long the hold will continue, or why the hold was put on the particular bill or confirmation request. If the issue still under a hold should be brought to the floor, the presiding officer can be almost certain of a *filibuster*. Some legislation is exempt from holds, typically a *continuing resolution* necessary to keep the government functioning. This is considered necessary legislation and cannot be stopped by individual senators.

MANAGING THE BILL ON THE FLOOR

The Senate and House do not have the same methods for managing bills on the floor. The different sizes of the membership—the Senate has only 100 members, whereas the House has 435 voting and 5 nonvoting members—are probably responsible for this more than any other factor. (Many other differences distinguish the two bodies, even the chambers in which they meet. The House chamber is the largest parliamentary room in the world; the Senate chamber is much smaller and more elegant, only 125 feet at its widest.[9])

"Unlike the Senate system of unanimous consent, which involves consultation between the leaders and interested senators on the terms of debate and amendment, the House had formalized this crucial gate keeping function in its Rules Committee."[10] At the time the bill is reported out of committee, the parliamentarian and members of the Rules Committee are involved in determining floor procedures for each piece of proposed legislation.[11]

The House Rules Committee, now functioning as a standing committee would, develops resolutions for bringing bills to the floor. Committee chairpersons and the sponsors of the measure request a rule from the Rules Committee. Such resolutions set the terms of debate and the numbers and types of amendments allowed. In a closed rule, only amendments suggested by the legislative committee reporting the bill will be considered. Open rules allow amendments, and there are several variations of rules controlling the processes and time limits.

At least one legislative day must ensue between the ruling and the consideration of the bill. The resolution to bring the bill to the floor includes the rulings, and it too must receive a majority vote. Members of the committee favorably reporting out a bill are fully involved in these procedures. Getting any major legislation passed seems to move at the speed of a glacier. At last count there were about 30 potential steps to the process.

Senators, at any time, can propose a motion that a bill be brought to the floor for consideration. A simple majority vote is all that is required to pass the motion. It is a duty of the committee chairman to report bills to the floor. Failing that, a majority of the members can force it out of committee. If a senator chooses to have no debate on the motion, the morning hour (before 2:00 P.M.) is the best time to bring it up.

At other times, the senator risks a filibuster and, perhaps, the seldom-successful vote for *cloture*. It is also possible the bill may die before it even receives consideration. "The most common way to bring up bills in the Senate is by unanimous consent."[12] It is also beyond doubt the safest way to seek passage.

Committees that have decided to not report out, or "sit on," a bill can find themselves affected by a seldom-used vote in the two chambers. In the House, the process—a discharge petition—requires the signatures of a majority. In the Senate, unanimous consent is necessary.

The bill in question is literally taken, or discharged, from the committee's jurisdiction. The potential for retaliation from committee members treated to a discharge petition is an unpleasant reality for those who engage in this method for forcing bills out of committees. Perhaps this is one explanation for its infrequent use.

Committee work does not end when a bill is successfully reported out but continues as long as the chamber has not disposed of the measure. Committee bill managers offering amendments are called upon first by the House Speaker. On the Senate floor, procedures are far less formal but outcomes are less predictable, too. Obviously, a single "no" vote by a senator wrecks a unanimous consent vote. Senators who oppose measures try to limit amendments or otherwise impede passage of bills.

When unanimous consent to bring forth the bill has been obtained in the Senate, the presiding officer calls for brief opening statements from both the majority and minority floor managers. Voting is by roll call. Both houses require that a majority of the committee be present to report a bill.

Unfriendly amendments are much more likely in the Senate. Unlike the rule in the House, a proposed amendment in the Senate does not have to relate to the subject of the bill itself. The House rule is called the *germaneness* rule. (An exception to this is that amendments must be germane when a general *appropriation* bill is being considered. Votes are taken immediately after a question of germaneness is posed. A majority is required for passage.)

House amendments must be germane, but in the Senate even entire bills, on completely different topics, can be added to any bill under consideration on the floor.[13] The now-infamous filibuster/cloture process is often called into play when this happens. The House does not allow filibusters and, therefore, has no need for a cloture rule.

As one might guess, the House has figured a way to get around a good many of its own rules. Committee members and their opponents have recourse to a method of bringing bills to the floor that allows them more freedom to maneuver. This is called suspension of the rules. This technique has gone through many changes, most recently under the Republican majority elected in the 104th Congress. Generally the committee desiring suspension of the rules sends a written request to the Speaker of the House.

The bills considered under this method do not allow more than $100 million in expenditures, and a suspension of rules generally forbids amendments on the floor of the House. Motions to suspend the rules can be made from the floor—with a caveat: it is the Speaker who must recognize members wishing to suspend the rules. It is not difficult to understand that this is one of the many times the speaker can exercise considerable power to forward the party's agenda.

CALENDARS

Not all legislation is created equal in Congress. Decisions must constantly be made about when to schedule debates on very different types of bills in each of the two chambers. This procedure is probably one of the most confusing to the public, and likely to many of the members as well. Calling on the expertise of the parliamentarians, the House Rules Committee, and members who have been in Congress a considerable length of time, the scheduling process may be the most complicated phase in the entire lawmaking process.

Once a committee has held hearings, done the markup on a bill, and reported it out to the whole membership—regardless of how well it has performed these tasks—the fate of all that work is still uncertain. For example, in the House there are five different lists, or *calendars*, on which a bill may be placed for subsequent action. For each day that a chamber is in session, a daily calendar is prepared and distributed to the members. Brief histories and summaries of the bills to be considered are included.

Bills are numbered in the order they are received from their respective committees. These numbers are used when bills are placed on the various calendars. Prior discussions among the leaders (minority and majority), with the help of experts available to Congress, clarify major points so that the bills normally reach the floor and debate ensues without too many surprises. The ideal is to call for consideration of the bill in its numerical order. As with almost every other function of Congress, however, this is not really the way things work. There are "privileged" bills, noncontroversial bills, discharge petitions, and money bills, all of which receive different treatment, some even being assigned their own special "day" or "hours."

Committee chairpersons are usually in charge of managing their bills, and they can be expected to be anxious about the scheduling process. The possibilities for twists and turns seem almost endless. Sometimes there are rules that must be followed and sometimes not. Bills under consideration can be returned to their committees or killed simply on procedural grounds. Some bills already placed on calendars are never called up for action.

Senators need to deal with only two calendars: one for treaty ratifications and nomination approvals and one for all other bills. Especially for treaty ratifications, the process can be handled by voice vote in just a few minutes. This assumes that a vote of unanimous consent, known as a *unanimous consent agreement*, has been passed.

Senators may bring up measures on the floor at any time. Rules of the Senate require that in order to make a motion, the senator must first obtain recognition from the presiding officer (always a member of the majority party). Senatorial tradition has been that refusal to recognize a colleague, either a fellow party member or one of the opposition, is a serious breach of etiquette. In spite of the recent erosion of this informal norm, many members still react strongly when it happens. Nonetheless, the majority leader is first among equals in questions of recognition on the Senate floor. He not only precedes all others seeking to be recognized, but also can move to table, or put off until later or maybe forever, a colleague's motion.

All senators have the opportunity to decide when to schedule legislation for debate on the floor. Unanimous consent is always preferred for making these decisions. Some standing rules guide behavior on the Senate floor, but there are far fewer rules than in the House. Attempting to reach unanimous consent in order not to invoke the rules is almost the norm. The standing rules can always be invoked should unanimous consent be unobtainable.

Senators can also avoid sending bills to a committee at all. This, too, can be achieved by unanimous consent.[14] Because Senate and House bills must be identical before being sent to the president, the Senate may avoid a tremendous amount of redundant activity by accepting House bills as written. If such a measure to accept a House bill is read twice on the floor, and unanimous consent cannot be reached, the bill is placed on the calendar and taken up so the entire Senate can debate and amend it.

Because the Senate must cover the same work as the House, but with fewer members, it is clear why senators look for ways to speed up the process. House rules require that reports and cost analyses accompany most bills. Similar Senate rules cover only appropriations measures. Avoiding the Senate's repetition of such a lengthy and costly process after the House has just completed it does seem to make sense.

The secret to the success of many of the shortcuts used in both the Senate and the House is the prior planning among their leaders. This advance work is carried out both before the legislation is assigned to committees and before it is assigned to a calendar. At that point, members can show their ability to cooperate, even though the planning session itself may be extremely partisan. After the leaders reach agreement, the docu-

During a January 1995 press conference, House Speaker Newt Gingrich holds up a copy of the Contract with America. The Republicans had gained a majority in the House of Representatives in the 1994 election, and the Contract was heralded to commit the legislators who signed it to reforming the federal government.

ments are read aloud on the Senate floor, recorded, and used thereafter to guide the debate. In the House, the usual procedure is first to send the bill to the Rules Committee.

Once scheduling decisions have been reached, members usually choose to go along with the agreements worked out by their leadership. The first session of the 104th Congress proved to be a bumpy one for the scheduling process, in the House of Representatives especially. The Contract with America was a scheduling priority and took a great deal of floor time. In addition to the large contingent of freshmen, a sizable number of members had served only one or two terms. Scheduling, as mentioned, requires experienced members and institutional memory to guide it. These were difficult to call into service with enthusiasm running so high among so many relatively inexperienced representatives. Committee work was minimal, and the process was difficult to control. There was a commitment to the idea of the Contract, but not sufficient preparation for the actual votes on the floor. In all, dealing with the Contract reinforced the value of experience gained over time in the complicated scheduling process.

CONFERENCE COMMITTEE REPORTS

Separate committees, in chambers whose procedures are sometimes quite different, are required by the Constitution to end up with identical language for prospective laws. In order to accomplish this, the conference committee has been a part of the process since the first Congress. In order for the two houses to hold a conference on bills that they have passed but that are not exactly alike, both chambers must agree. The Senate can do so by voice vote, the House by an approval of the full committee or by obtaining a resolution from the Rules Committee.

Appointments to conference committees are made by the presiding officer in the Senate and the speaker of the House. Customarily, their choices are those submitted to them by chairpeople of the committees proposing the bills (both majority and minority members serve). The House has passed a rule to formalize the process: "The Speaker shall name members who are primarily responsible for the legislation and shall, to the fullest extent possible, include the principal proponents of the major provisions of the bill as it passed the House.[15]

Conference committees often suffer from having too many members. Agreements become correspondingly difficult to reach. There is no formal limit to the numbers of conferees who can be appointed but there must be a minimum of three. Unless the full House votes otherwise, the conference is held in open meetings. Discussions of defense and intelligence bills are, however, normally closed.

Conference committees offer the last chance to change decisions made during consideration on the floor. Arguments over controversial issues are notorious. This is only to be expected, because conferees are selected from the same committees that reported the proposals in the first place. At this point, compromise is not only desirable but also essential. A bill can die in conference if the members cannot come to agreement. It will also die if the sessions ends before work on the measure is completed.

Each house has already passed its own bill by a majority. In a conference to reconcile two different bills covering the same jurisdictions, each chamber is allowed only one vote. Again, this decision must be made by a majority of a conference committee of the two Congressional branches. That majority is aware that bills reported from a conference are safe from amendment: none is permitted on the floor of either chamber.

When the conference committee has successfully completed its work, the staff prepares a conference report that is signed by a majority of the conferees. This is the document that is reported out and is subject to final up-or-down vote in the two chambers. These reports are brought to the floor as privileged bills and are not required to go through the House Rules Committee. Because bills are often considered in several different units, the conferees will sometimes ask for a rule to guide the discussion on the floor of the House.

Passage of bills coming from conference committees is not certain, but the chances are very good. All the work that has gone into the measure, both behind-the-scenes and in open negotiations, has involved a great deal of time and effort. It has also involved many members of the majority and minority and their staffs. If the bill is passed, it is signed by leaders of both houses and sent to the president. Should it be voted down, the measure can be sent to a newly constituted conference committee, or a new bill covering the same issues can be introduced at a later date.

Chapter 3

LEADERSHIP

*The future lies with those wise political leaders
who realize that the great public is interested
more in government than in politics.*
—FRANKLIN D. ROOSEVELT, 1940

Many years of hard work have been the traditional route to
leadership in Congress. Working out solutions to national problems takes a vast amount of harmony and civility. Accomplish-
ing this requires frequent blurring of political party lines,
sincere cooperation between senators and representatives, and
a thorough understanding of the way their institution functions.

According to the *Washington Post*'s David S. Broder, "The
need for cross-party friendships is even greater now than in the
past, because the ideological differences between the parties
have grown. And in both the House and Senate, a bloodless version of 'ethnic cleansing' has been taking place within each
party." Broder believes that the "companionship that once
crossed party lines in Congress . . . has been replaced by a tone
of unremitting enmity."[1]

With Congress in such a state of partisan acrimony, the
balance of power is extremely lop-sided between the minority
and majority leaders. Minority leaders do have powers spelled
out in standing rules, and the majority party cannot infringe
upon those.

Voters have determined the Congressional majority in the

most recent elections. From time to time, however, the public's displeasure with the majority serves to lessen the minority's disadvantages between elections. In a climate such as today's, though, leadership is mainly partisanship.

The two national parties have established, in both chambers, policy committees that have no legislative authority. They serve the needs of the majority leadership. Members who serve on policy committees have a professional staff to assist them in advancing the party's agenda. There are very few independents or other party representatives among the leaders of Congress. Although those members are not excluded from chairing committees or becoming top officials, they simply don't have enough votes among their colleagues to overtake Democratic or Republican candidates for the posts.

Democratic and Republican policy committees clarify the party leadership's positions on issues for both the members of Congress and the public. Information gathering and dissemination are among their most important functions. Party agenda meetings, newsletters, periodic bulletins, seminars, radio and television programs, and most recently the Internet have all been conduits for information from House and Senate Democratic and Republican policy committees.

Service on a policy committee is in addition to the duties required for regular Congressional committees. For handling the business of the nation, the Senate Republicans (whether they are the minority or majority in Congress) have seven top party leadership positions: floor leader, assistant floor leader (called the whip), chairperson of the Republican Policy Committee, chairperson of the Republican Conference (which nominates members for leadership posts), secretary of the Conference, chairperson of the Republican Senatorial Campaign Committee, and chairman of the Republican Committee on Committees (which nominates committee chairpeople.)[2]

Rules changes over the last two decades have had a strong impact on the selection of leaders in Congress. In both chambers, the membership now votes on the nominations of office seekers. These nominations are made at a party *caucus* before the Congressional session opens. This change has made Congress more egalitarian, as leaders are now subject to peer approval.

In Article I of the Constitution, the vice president of the United States is designated as President of the Senate. This is a position in name only, unless a tiebreaking vote is required. The presiding officer of the Senate (a temporary honor) is selected by the majority leader and serves as he or she directs. This Senate President "pro tempore," as the Constitution calls the substitute presiding officer, is given no special powers when he or she is not presiding over the Senate chamber.

The House of Representatives differs in several very significant ways. For that chamber, the Constitution states simply that members are to select their own Speaker (without saying how), and the first one was dutifully chosen in 1789. It has become a remarkable, perhaps unique, governmental position. Assisting the Speaker in leadership functions are the majority (or floor) leader, minority floor leader, majority and minority whips, and the party committee chairpersons.

The term *leadership* actually has several meanings when used in connection with the U.S. Congress. Mentioned above are the top officials. Within the last quarter century, strict adherence to a tradition of seniority has weakened. Over that time, the notion of leadership has been expanded to include not only chairpersons of full committees but those of subcommittees as well. "Congressional history, it is worth noting, demonstrates that centralized authority is not a permanent condition in either chamber; rather, the forces of centralization versus decentralization are constantly in play, and they regularly adjust and reconfigure in response to new conditions and circumstances."[3] There is no question, however, that the Speaker is "king of the hill."

THE SPEAKER

According to Judith Bentley, "Far more than merely presiding, . . . the Speaker must pull diverse people and views together to reach at least a momentary consensus. Most of that work goes

Sam Rayburn (D-Texas) served as Speaker of the House for 17 years (1940–47, 1949–53, 1955–61). As the leader of the House of Representatives, the Speaker wields much power and is considered the second most powerful person in the United States.

on out of the chair and off the floor, in the Speaker's lobby and offices, the hallways and conference rooms. Order comes from the chair; power is more diffuse."[4]

Indicating the uniqueness of the Speaker's role, the Speaker performs the following official functions, among others:

1. Nominates majority party members of Rules Committee (responsible for all major bills and scheduling)
2. Takes "complete charge of measures considered under the suspension procedure"[5]
3. Chairs party unit that makes committee assignments
4. Appoints colleague to preside over House sitting as "Committee of the Whole" (does favors by giving even junior members recognition)
5. Votes as tiebreaker on major legislation
6. Names primary committee in multiple referrals of bills; determines time limits and so forth
7. Recognizes (or denies) members seeking to make motions during sessions
8. Appoints task forces and commissions (more favors)
9. Appoints members of select and conference committees (assigns power to others)
10. Calls roll instead of using electronic system for voting (perhaps to stall)
11. Determines if and when measures come to floor for consideration
12. Follows the vice president in line of presidential succession

These are just some of the formal privileges allowed the Speaker. Despite the requirement that some of the Speaker's choices for certain committees be approved by the other members, it is safe to say the Speaker's choices are likely to be accepted.

The personal power that can be exercised in this office cannot be calculated with any accuracy. Over time there have been Speakers who, with little opposition, really "ran the show." It is no wonder the Speaker is considered the second most powerful person in the United States after the president.

$\mathscr{A}$SSIGNING MEMBERS TO COMMITTEES

From the very first Congress in 1789, the methods for choosing committee members have changed over and over. Growth alone would demand that the committee system be adjusted to reflect the increasing amount of work which must be done. Certain committees have become very powerful, affecting the numbers of members who desire seats on them. It is no exaggeration that committees are "the most important point of access to Congress for outsiders, . . . interest groups, the administration, and the general public."[6]

The four major Congressional power groups, Senate Democrats and Republicans and House Democrats and Republicans, are responsible for choosing committee members. The simplest way to refer to the four units they select for this job is as the committees on committees. Although they have different names, they all do the same thing: make nominations for committee posts each congressional session. Although the written rules say the full congressional memberships are to elect members of committees, it is really done by a limited group of the parties' leaders. The lists drawn up by party leaders in the committees on committees are generally ratified by each house.

Between election day in November and the first day of the new session in January, the committees on committees (their exact makeup is determined by slightly different methods in each group) meet to decide on their nominations for leaders and committee members. The entire party caucus and then the full membership of each chamber must approve the nominations. In the House, the leader of each party chairs the committee on committees. Senators may choose to follow that procedure, but it is not required.

Soon after they are sworn in, members receive their committee assignments. Unless the majority of Congress changes, the rosters of committees are much the same from Congress to Congress. Periodically, one chamber or the other changes a name or drops or adds a committee. These changes are reflected in the assignments of members.

As with most functions, the Senate's methods of assigning members to committees are less complicated than those in the House. Sizes and jurisdictions of committees are written into the standing rules. The ratios of minority and majority party members on each committee are not spelled out in Senate rules but rather are decided by negotiations among the leaders of both parties. Generally they reflect the ratios of chamber memberships. The House committee ratios, too, generally tend to be close to those of the full chamber.

Senators and Representatives divide their committees into several different levels. "[T]he current system concentrates power not in the chairmen of many committees as before, but in virtually all the members of a few elite committees."[7] Senators are supposed to serve on only two "major" committees. In the House such a committee would be called "exclusive," and a representative can serve on only one of these. Appropriations, Rules, and Ways and Means Committees are the three exclusive committees.

All one hundred senators are guaranteed a seat on one of the four major committees—Appropriations, Armed Services, Finance, and Foreign Relations—before any member is given a seat on two of them. "This rule prevented senior members from monopolizing these important committee posts and facilitated the appointment of relatively junior senators much earlier in their career [sic] than had previously been possible."[8] Senators are supposed to be limited to two major and one minor committee, but it appears the exceptions are more frequent than the rule.

Competition for certain seats can be very heated. When several members are seeking a seat on the same committee on which there are not enough openings, seniority is generally the deciding factor. It often happens that the leadership will decide to expand memberships rather than disappoint a member. Committee size is entirely up to the discretion of the leadership in each chamber. Very rarely is a member taken off a committee involuntarily. Called a property right, this norm exists in both chambers and among both parties. A member can retain a committee seat as long as he or she desires.

From time to time, either house may adopt a rule limiting the number of terms members can serve on certain committees. This prevents personal resentment when a member reaches the term limit and must choose another committee on which to serve. Campaigns for these open posts can become very lively, involving powerful local leaders, lobbyists, committee chairpersons, and anyone else whose endorsement might sway the decision of the party chiefs.

Leaders definitely want to provide committee assignments desired by their fellow party members. Frequently, reelection chances of members are enhanced by the committee assignments they are able to procure. Constituents are aware of the power accruing to their representatives when they notice the services provided to their districts. Power to provide special services and benefits to constituents comes through careful work on legislation in committees, not from merely being elected to Congress or showing debating skills on the floor.

Staying on the same committee is the most likely way a member eventually becomes chairperson. Changing to a different committee puts a member at the bottom of that list. Although the use of seniority for appointing committee chairpersons is no longer strictly followed, it is still the case that senior members most frequently move into those positions of power. Each committee of more than 15 members must now have at least four subcommittees. (This also changes from time to time.)

Subcommittee chairpersons have gained more and more power over the past two decades since the so-called "subcommittee bill of rights" was put into effect. These reforms changed many of the power centers in the Congress. No longer could the long-powerful coalition of conservative Southern Democrat and Republican committee chairpersons keep legislation that they disapproved of bottled up in their committees.

Reform movements are often attempted in Congress, but the one occurring in the early to mid-1970s was successful in several important aspects. Its main impact was to break the power block against liberalizing legislation. Limits on the types of committee assignments allowed to each member, increased numbers of subcommittees, and staffing allowances were among the most important changes. Seniority is the still the norm for selecting chairpersons of the more than 200 subcommittees, but power in Congress is now more evenly divided. Even junior members now have more opportunities to influence legislation than before the reforms were passed.

An incident in October 1995 shows how junior members took on the Republican leadership and succeeded. "Responding to angry House Republican backbenchers, GOP leaders indicated yesterday that a freshman rebel disciplined Wednesday for voting against a major appropriations bill would be offered a choice committee assignment to make amends. The sudden turn in the fortunes of Rep. Mark W. Neumann (R-Wisconsin) was another dramatic illustration of the unprecedented power of the huge block of first- and second-term members of the new, Republican-controlled House."[9] Neumann had been told he was being reassigned from the Appropriations Subcommittee on National Security to a much less prestigious one. His fellow freshmen rebelled. Neumann retained his Appropriations subcommittee assignment and was given a seat on the powerful Budget Committee![10]

Chapter 4

OTHER INFLUENCES INSIDE COMMITTEES

Every country is renewed out of the unknown ranks and not out of the ranks of those already famous and powerful and in control.
—WOODROW WILSON, 1912

Besides the committee members themselves, other individuals and groups affect congressional committees. Let's take a look at the roles that committee staff, employees, lobbyists, the executive branch, courts, and the media play in the committee process.

STAFF

Increasing numbers of committees and subcommittees continued to create more work for each member, until finally additional staff became a necessity. Some analysts believe that staff are now actually the ones doing most of the work of legislating.

A staff member of a Senate committee (right) prepares for a hearing. Some observers believe that today's committee staffers do much of the work of legislating.

Popular opinion holds that congressional staffers are driven by ambition and willing to work incredible hours under less than wonderful conditions for modest pay, just to be near the power center of Washington, D.C.

While that may be true of some, most nonclerical staff hired to work on committees are professionals with extensive education and training. Committee work often requires special knowledge that only thorough, wide-ranging experience can provide. Staff positions are established by rules in both the Senate and House, and the funds to hire staff (both clerical and professional) are provided from budgets separate from those for members' offices. There are also separate staff for the home and Washington offices of each senator and representative.

Committee staff frequently do work in cooperation with the personal Congressional staff, but serve under the direction of committee chairpersons. Limited numbers of staff are selected by the chairpersons of subcommittees, also. Among the official duties of the committee staffs are original research, policy question clarification, selecting witnesses and organizing hearings, briefing and drawing up questions for the committee, drafting amendments during markup, analyzing potential costs and impacts on existing legislation, preparing members for managing bills on the floor, and presenting the issues to the public through the media. In essence, the committee staffs deal with every phase of lawmaking except introducing the original proposal and voting on the final version. Staff even accompany senators onto the floor during sessions. This practice is not permitted in the House, however.

These highly skilled individuals also keep in touch with federal agencies, interest groups, and members of the media to stay informed about professional and public opinions. Lobbyists, and occasionally the courts, use instructions prepared by staff and included with the final bill reports to clarify ambiguities in the bill's language. Certain investigations require very special expertise. For that purpose, committees are authorized to hire temporary staff. The privilege of handpicking staff is one of the powerful rewards given to committee chairpersons.

NONLEGISLATIVE EMPLOYEES

Congress has long excluded itself from fair labor laws. Were it not for the fact that the Constitution permits it to make its own rules, Congress long ago would have been in violation of the very laws it has imposed on other employers. Capitol Hill employees—such as police, cafeteria workers, and mail clerks—have only recently won some of the same employee rights as other workers in the nation.

With the passage of the Congressional Accountability Act early in 1996, Congress finally must itself adhere to the some of the laws it has ignored for some of its own helpers. Staffers are not covered by most fair standards laws, and the recent law still excludes them. "Senior House members and Senate officials have balked at proposed rules allowing congressional staff members to form unions, contending that large numbers of employees should be excluded because of sensitive positions and potential conflicts of interest."[1] The feared conflicts, according to certain members, would be between union loyalty and loyalty to members for whom the staffers work. From all reports, there is still a lot to be done before these issues are settled to the satisfaction of workers on Capitol Hill.

$\mathcal{L}$OBBYISTS

Members constantly protest that they must campaign virtually nonstop. It is important to note, however, that Congress seems to find this burdensome until the opportunity to reform campaign financing becomes a serious possibility. "The Senate yesterday killed a bipartisan bill to overhaul Congress's campaign finance laws, dashing already dim chances for a successful end this year to the 25-year drive to curb spending and special-interest influence on House and Senate elections."[2]

Failing in an attempt at cloture, the Senate "fell six votes short of the 60 needed to cut off a GOP-led filibuster and to put the legislation on track for passage."[3] This failure is even more revealing as it was a Republican, Senator John McCain of Arizona, who was the main sponsor of the reform measure. Also, both President Clinton and Speaker Gingrich had pledged to call together a bipartisan commission to work out a solution to the problem. According to Senate leader Trent Lott (R-Mississippi), reform of campaign laws "is too important to address right at this point in the heat of the national election campaign."[4] Does Congress really want campaign reform? Not yet, evidently.

Lobbyists, purported to have unlimited amounts of money available for campaign contributions, are considered responsible for the constant campaign fund-raising. One very important point needs to be made in this regard: *Most* lobbyists do not

In 1995, Senator John McCain (R-Arizona) sponsored an unsuccessful bill that sought to reform campaign financing. Congress has not shown a willingness to enact campaign reform laws.

spend great sums trying to influence lawmakers. Their job— and it is essential—is to provide information. Even with increased staffing and funds for investigation, it is impossible for legislators to keep up with all the important issues concerning the nation. In any controversial issue, there are at least two sides. Lobbyists on opposing sides gather and release facts to support their positions, thereby promoting a more open, informed discussion of the controversy.

Some lobbying groups, however, do spend large sums, and their influence is obvious. Until Congress decides to pass reform laws addressing this problem, the voters will watch bemused while members of Congress profess they do not want to campaign all the time, yet can't seem to muster the votes to change things.

EXECUTIVE BRANCH

Companion bills (duplicates of proposed legislation) are sent to the Senate and House directly from various agencies of the federal government. It is not necessary for all these bills to go to committees. Some can be placed immediately on each chamber's calendars.

Committees do receive some legislative proposals directly from the executive branch and consider these in the same manner as those created by members of Congress. The rest of the process is the same: in the House, the bill goes to the Rules Committee; in the Senate's less formal system, the bill is introduced from the floor by a member agreeing to sponsor the legislation.

COURTS

No matter how carefully legislation is written, it is impossible to foresee what confusions might arise or what phrasing might later appear to be vague. On some issues, vague wording may even have been used intentionally. In such situations, the courts must decide intent when the law is challenged. Interest groups and private citizens who need interpretations must appeal to the judiciary branch of government for help. The courts use instructions contained in the final committee reports as the major evidence of congressional intent.

HE MEDIA

All congressional committee meetings open to the public are also open to the media. Although hundreds of meetings are held during every session and receive no media attention, when a controversial bill is being marked up or when sensitive hearings are in progress, media coverage is inevitable. Allowing television and radio coverage in committee meetings is perhaps the most significant change in the recent history of congressional committees.

Press photographers attend a Senate Judiciary Committee hearing in 1996. Media coverage of committee meetings and hearings helps voters keep track of what Congress and their representatives are doing.

Chapter 5

COMMITTEES
AND THE
BUDGET
PROCESS

The budget is a mythical bean bag. Congress votes
mythical beans into it, and then tries to reach in
and pull real beans out.
— The Autobiography of Will Rogers (1949)

Responsibility for raising and spending money to run the government of the United States is vested in the Congress. Understanding the congressional budget process is not impossible, but it is hardly light reading. Its very complexity invites criticism from all sides.

Public unhappiness with Congress generally falls into two main categories: it taxes too much and it spends too much. What has become very clear is that the government has too many debts. Were the federal government to be given an allowance today and never again exceed it, the costs for just the interest on the government's excess spending (national debt) during the past fifty years would continue to be staggering. (The figure is now hovering around $5 trillion.)

48

Each year that the income of the country is less than the amount spent, there is an annual deficit. When all the annual deficits are totaled, the figure is the national debt. Congress sets debt limits by law but repeatedly finds itself having to raise the limit to avoid violating the very laws it has created. No one is happy with this state of affairs. Some of the bitterest fights in Washington are over this issue.

One of the problems is that laws passed by former Congresses have established programs considered more or less perpetual, such as Social Security, pensions for government employees, and Medicare. These programs, called entitlements, have been placed outside annual budget considerations. Yet, along with defense and a few smaller programs, they represent nearly 70 percent of all funds spent every year by the United States. Spending for these programs is mandated; that is, their funding is not revised each year after being reviewed by congressional committees.

The huge entitlement programs were established to run without needing an annual budget review. Also, the government pays for those programs even if annual payroll tax contributions for the programs do not cover their costs. "Unlike defense or domestic discretionary programs—for which the Appropriations committees recommend annual amounts and which all lawmakers may vote on—entitlement spending occurs automatically under the terms outlined in the statute. . . . Dominating the scene are the benefits offered to the elderly."[1]

Interest groups, which often have very large memberships, do not want cuts in funds for entitlement programs that benefit them. A number of these programs were created for very good reasons, and some are part of a successful democracy. U.S. citizens are noted for belonging to a number of different interest groups. This is a dilemma for those in Congress who would like to make immediate and drastic changes: They risk being sent home permanently by unhappy voters.

Buddy MacKay (R-Florida) has noted, "The real policy decisions of the next decade are going to be centered at Ways and Means—Medicare financing, Social Security entitlements. . . . Long-term health care for the elderly is the next regularly sched-

In 1968, Helen McFarland (left) and Luther Smith hold up their Social Security checks, which were the first two checks received after a 1968 payment increase. Social Security is among the various entitlement programs placed outside the federal government's annual budget considerations.

uled crisis."[2] The elderly make up an increasingly large segment of our population.

Another side to the controversy was pointed out by Ellen Miller in her column, "Tax Wars" in *The Hill*. According to columnist Miller, "If you ask the average middle-class taxpayer what these terms mean—capital gains rollover, safe-harbor provision, passive foreign investment, possession credit, minimum alternative—chances are you'll get a blank stare. But these tax-code provisions have a great deal of importance for another sector of society: They mean big tax savings for wealthy individuals and large corporations."[3]

From the days of its very first session, Congress has constructed an increasingly elaborate and complex system for the federal government's budget process. Yet members of the legislative branch do not actually start it; the executive branch does. The president first outlines his policies. With assistance from many sources, especially the Office of Management and Budget and the Council of Economic Advisors, executive agencies send recommendations to the president covering annual budgets, which include projections for at least the following four years.

Every year, presidential proposals for the government's budget take up several volumes. Estimates from prior budget projections are compared with the actual taxing and spending for the *fiscal year* just completed. In this way, annual performances are continuously compared to see whether targets are being met.

Congress even has an official calendar for the process. Al-

A courier carries copies of President Bill Clinton's fiscal 1996 federal budget. The Presidential budget proposals are sent to Congress in February, and a budget bill enacted by Congress must be signed by the end of the government's fiscal year in September.

though the steps may not always be completed on time, the process begins when the president's budget is sent to Congress during the first week of February. (This is the proposed budget for a year and a half in the future.) All of the steps are supposed to be completed and the budget bill signed by the Congress and the president no later than September 30, the last day of the government's fiscal year.

Congress is not obliged to accept the president's budget proposals. Congressional committees concerned with the budget (and there are few that are not) have not been idle while the federal bureaucracy and the president have been drawing up their budget proposals. Assisted by the Congressional Budget Office, the Joint Committees on Taxation and Economics, and other committees, Congress draws up its own annual budget plan.

Any part of the president's budget is subject to change by congressional committees. Funding and taxing levels can be changed, and programs can be added or eliminated. As mentioned, this budget includes only about a third of the total sums spent by the government. Committees spend much of their time in hearings, analyzing past and current income and spending, writing amendments, and marking up bills.

Every committee affected by the president's proposals must produce budget plans for programs that fall within their jurisdictions. These plans are sent to the Budget Committees of each chamber. (The Budget & Impoundment Control Act of 1974, which established the Budget Committees, specifically included membership rotation in the law. Although membership time limits have been adjusted, rotation is still part of the standing rules. This is designed to ensure that no single member becomes too powerful in budget matters.) Budget Committees then pull all these plans together. The result is a concurrent resolution for each chamber. The resolutions from the House and Senate Budget Committees must be presented to the full chambers for a vote and eventually to a conference committee, which comes up with a single plan.

This vote produces the congressional policy document, which includes budgetary totals and guides the taxing and spending committees in methods to achieve their goals. These are working documents only. Concurrent resolutions are not law and are not sent to the president for signature. The president will, however, eventually have to sign the legislation arising from the annual budget, so Congress definitely has an interest in considering the president's policies and budget proposals along with its own plan.

The "Concurrent Resolution on the Budget for Fiscal Year 1997" was submitted to the Committee of the Whole House on May 14, 1996. Report 104-575 of the second session of the 104th Congress contains nearly 500 pages of fine print. Included in the resolution from the House are many references to the recent struggles between the Republican-led Congress and the Democratic president. A point-by-point rebuttal of each of the 82 reasons the president gave for vetoing the balanced budget proposed by the Congress is included. Resolutions are obviously flexible and not just about numbers.

In the budgeting process, problems frequently arise because the Office of Management and Budget (the main executive branch fiscal adviser) and the Congressional Budget Office (the main Congressional fiscal adviser) do not always work from the same sets of assumptions. One major difference is that the president's advisers are expressly working on a plan to carry out the president's policies. On the other hand, the Congressional Budget Office assists committees that have both majority and minority party representation and differing policies. From time to time, majority and minority are reversed in one or both of the houses of Congress. Therefore, figures used by the Congressional Budget Office are inclined to be more conservative or, in the view of some observers, less optimistic. The results can be very different projections for income and expenses. This problem is especially pronounced when the president and the majority in Congress are not of the same political party.

Each chamber, as usual, has different methods for dealing with this part of the process. Some of the Senate's most honored traditions, however, are set aside during budgetary voting. Debate on concurrent resolutions is allowed for only 50 hours—not the usual filibuster/cloture proceeding. Also, any amendments to the resolutions must be germane, as amendments in the House must be at all times. Rules of the House permit resolving into the Committee of the Whole, making a majority easier to obtain on the floor.

Congressional committees must take into consideration laws that already exist, making sure that nothing in the new budget will conflict with them. To accomplish this, a procedure called *reconciliation* became law in the 1974 Budget Act. (The Congressional Budget Office was created by this Act.) If committees find that existing laws must be changed in order to avoid conflicts with the current budget, the necessary changes are supposed to be identified no later than June 15 each year. These changes must be laid out in detail, agreed to, and then incorporated into the budget bill.

Several very important laws mandating deficit reduction and cuts in government spending have been enacted since 1974. Targets for eliminating the deficit, which were set out in some of these laws, were not met. Recent increases in the national debt and reductions in funds available for annual federal expenditures, have had serious impacts upon the way the committees in Congress handle taxing and spending.

Two powerful standing committees are in the forefront of legislation for the U.S. budget: the House Committee on Ways and Means and the House Committee on Appropriations. The first raises the money, the latter does most of the spending. More precisely, the Appropriations Committee begins the process of spending; the federal agencies are the actual spenders.

THE HOUSE COMMITTEE ON WAYS AND MEANS

When this country was born, it was already in debt. First among its benefactors were its own citizens, who were former subjects of the British crown. Any contributors to the cause, including European governments, banks, private companies, and citizens, were eagerly welcomed. The revolutionaries became their debtors.

In its very first year, Congress established an ad hoc committee (made up of a member from each state having ratified the Constitution) whose instructions were to look into questions of raising money to supply the new nation. This was the first Committee on Ways and Means.

That committee lasted only a short time and was superseded in its duties by the Treasury Department under Secretary Alexander Hamilton. Then in December 1801, the House adopted a resolution establishing a standing committee, again named the Committee on Ways and Means. Raising money, paying debts, and supplying the federal government were now all part of the duties of the new committee. This was the situation for more than 60 years.

In 1865, the committee's duties were split between raising money and spending it. Ways and Means became the primary money gatherer. For some time, too, the committee was also the unit that appointed members to other House committees. Along with Appropriations, Ways and Means has always been considered either the most, or second-most, desirable committee on which to serve.

Among its former members have been presidents, vice presidents, House speakers, Supreme Court judges, and presidential cabinet members. Even abbreviated details of the committee's jurisdiction take up six single-spaced pages. The first enumerated duty is "Federal revenue measures generally. The Committee on Ways and Means has the responsibility for raising the revenue required to finance the Federal Government. This includes individual and corporate income taxes, excise taxes, estate taxes, gift taxes, and other miscellaneous taxes."[4] The document goes on to say that the Committee has jurisdiction over the authority of the federal government to borrow money, which also includes adjusting the debt ceiling. Add to that Social Security, trade and tariff laws, health care including Medicare, and it is not difficult to understand why this is a very powerful committee. It touches, in some way, almost all U.S. citizens.

The 104th Congress's House Ways and Means Committee has a membership of 21 Republicans and 15 Democrats. Chair-

Representative Bill Archer (R-Texas) is chairman of the House Ways and Means Committee. This important committee is responsible for raising the money required to operate the federal government.

man of the full committee is Bill Archer (R-Texas). Samuel M. Gibbons (D-Florida) is the ranking minority member. Indicating the vast jurisdiction of the committee is the diversity of its five standing subcommittees: Health, Human Resources, Oversight, Social Security, and Trade.

Today, the main committee room of Ways and Means is Room #1100 in the Longworth House Office Building. The room definitely reflects the prestige of the committee. A magnificent carved oak dais, bristling with microphones, covers the entire front of the room. Each committee member's seat is identified, and staff seats are close by. Behind the dais and on the opposite wall hang deep blue velvet draperies decorated with gold tassels. Thick, dark blue carpeting muffles all sounds except those of bells announcing votes on the floor of the House.

Imposing portraits honoring former chairmen hang in large gilt frames on two of the walls. Sconces and artfully designed indirect lighting add to the feeling of elegance. When preparing to consider the country's money issues, it is here the committee and staff (often more staff than members) are hosts to administrators of federal programs, special interest witnesses, and public citizens.

Article I, section 7, of the U.S. Constitution states: "all Bills for raising Revenue shall originate in the House of Representatives." Rules of the House require that the committee prepare "recommendations as to the appropriate level of the public debt which would then be set forth in the concurrent resolution on the budget and serve as the basis for an increase or decrease in the statutory limit on the debt."[5]

Written rules state that the full committee must meet at least once each month—(every second Wednesday while the House is in session). Ratios for majority and minority members on each subcommittee are also set out in written rules, as are the jurisdictional boundaries of each one. In the case of the Subcommittee on Oversight, in "matters involving the Internal Revenue Code and other revenue issues" the full committee shares the jurisdiction with the smaller unit.

The Joint Economic Committee, comprised of ten senators and ten representatives (the majority party has six members and the minority party four members in each committee), was established to help both the House Ways and Means Committee and its counterpart, the Senate Committee on Finance. This is one of the four joint committees serving both chambers. (The Joint Committee on Taxation is also an invaluable source

The House Ways and Means Committee holds a meeting. Ways and Means handles bills affecting taxes and tariffs.

of help. Its major focus is the Internal Revenue Service.) Expert staff conducts studies of issues involving federal policy. Although it has no legislative authority, the Joint Economic Committee does hold hearings and publishes its findings.

Income taxes have not always been with us, nor have corporate taxes. Most of the country's early revenues came from trade: charges on imports, excise taxes, and income from selling land. Fluctuating economic conditions frequently stimulate changes in income tax laws. Today, taxes on income account for about 45 percent of all our country's receipts. Because of the origin of the Social Security and Medicare programs, taxes funding them are acquired through company payrolls and have increased dramatically in the past few decades. Not only has the number of workers gone up, but the tax rate has also been raised by Congress. However, all indications are that in the future these two enormous programs will be too expensive as they are now organized and will not have enough funds to operate. Congress and the administration have not come to an agreement on how to solve this problem.

The Ways and Means Committee is supposed to be the only committee reporting bills affecting taxes and tariffs. For decades past and to this day, the House considers tax measures under closed rules (no amendments), agreeing with Wilbur D. Mills (D-Arkansas), chairman of the Ways and Means Committee from 1959 to 1974, that tax legislation was too complex and technical to be tampered with on the floor. If unlimited floor amendments were allowed, Mills argued, "the internal revenue code soon would be in shambles and at the mercy of pressure groups."[6]

According to Walter Oleszek, "A controversial rule adopted at the start of the GOP-controlled 104th Congress requires a three-fifths (rather than a simple majority) vote to pass measures containing an income tax rate increase."[7] Introduction of an amendment that has not been approved in the Rules Committee would require unanimous consent, an unlikely outcome in such a large and diverse membership as the House of Representatives or even in the smaller Committee of the Whole. Many alternative plans for increasing the income side of the equation are received from a multitude of sources. The staff analyzes them and explores the possibilities for better budgeting.

In the budget process, once hearings have been conducted and budget targets set, federal agencies are informed of the totals that they will be permitted to spend. This step is called *authorization* and generally must precede the next step, appropriation.

Adding to the confusion at budget time is the fact that not all programs can survive with short-term budgeting. Some budgets are for one year, others two years, some five, and several are given no time or funding limits at all (Social Security, for example). This is the main reason Congress cannot simply sit down, decide how much money it will likely take in each year, set a plan for how to spend the funds, and give the money to the agencies to spend.

Nor is it possible for Ways and Means to accurately calculate the nation's income for the year ahead or the eventual costs of programs and supplies. A lot of very hard work goes into trying to forecast these totals. The experts do not make guesses; the totals they are looking for are "moving targets."

The country now spends more than it takes in each year, and the deficits grow. One economic theory is that there are good reasons for the government to borrow money. If the benefits for the future are obvious, this theory goes, it makes sense to provide for them, even if some of today's costs are covered by credit instead of cash.

Congressional committees in the 104th session were not permitted to rely on credit. This is called the PAYGO system, derived from the phrase "pay-as-you-go." If a committee wants to fund something that exceeds budget limits, it must take money from other programs. Systems for "score keeping" are very complicated and are constantly challenged and changed. The goal, however, is clear: to have income and outflow equal; that is, a balanced budget. For the Committee on Ways and Means, overseeing the income side of the equation is the challenge. For controlling the spending side, the focus moves to another committee.

THE HOUSE COMMITTEE ON APPROPRIATIONS

In 1865, when Congress removed the duties of spending from the Ways and Means Committee, it established the House Committee on Appropriations. The committee's history has not been smooth. Its jurisdiction, the ever-important aspect of a committee, has contracted more times than expanded. According to James A. Thurber of American University, "The final blow occurred in 1885, when the authority to report six more appropriations bills—for the army, consular affairs, Indian affairs, military academy, naval affairs, and post office—was taken away and given to various legislative committees with jurisdiction over these matters."[8]

Nonetheless, despite many reforms House Appropriations is still considered one of the two most powerful committees in Congress. Under the tight budget conditions of the last two decades, Appropriations has retained and even reinforced its reputation for being the main watchdog over the nation's purse.

Perhaps the finest view of the heart of the nation's capital is through the soaring windows of the Appropriations Committee chairman's office. Quiet elegance is the only way to describe the room, one of three beautifully appointed rooms housing the full committee's leader and staff. Originally assigned to the Speaker of the House of Representatives, the suite of offices is just off the corridor leading to the House floor.

Functionally, the Committee on Appropriations is not exactly one committee. Its 13 subcommittees are the centers of power. Each subcommittee has been assigned its own offices and has its own staff of professionals with years of experience in federal budgeting. Richard Munson's fascinating book, *The Cardinals of Capitol Hill*, points out one of the major powers the chairpersons of the 13 subcommittees enjoy. Normal procedure in the House is for the Rules Committee and committee chairs to set the methods under which bills will be managed on the floor. The 13 "cardinals" can skip this step altogether, choosing their own time to bring measures to the floor. When they choose to go through the Rules Committee, they can decide whether amendments will be allowed, if members will be prohibited from striking certain sections of bills, how long debate will last, even if points of order will be acceptable.

The Appropriations and Ways and Means committees are supposed to have separate functions. Nonetheless, turf wars between the two are not unusual. The basis of these wars is the difficulty in separating "authorizing" from "appropriating." Authorizing functions affect grand totals. Appropriations cover the "what, where, and how much for each" categories of dividing up the annual budget.

Many legislative committees have the power to develop programs and plan for future expenditures. Only appropriations committees can give actual permission to federal agencies to purchase the government's services and supplies. The first part of the annual two-step budget process, authorization, determines the bottom-line totals that may be spent. These totals are sent to House and Senate appropriations committees, which then divide up the totals among already established categories of government expenses (usually 20 categories). These categories were developed primarily to assist the appropriations committee staffs in identifying legislative committee jurisdictions.

Considering that the Constitution enumerates congressional duties and written rules further interpret them, the additional six-step process that the budget proposals must go through—(1) starting with the president's policy plan, (2) going through federal agencies' financial officers, (3) arriving in legislative committees, (4) moving on to the Budget Committees, (5) traveling to the two chambers for a concurrent resolution debate and vote, and finally, (6) ending up in the Appropriations Committee—would seem to ensure that there could not possibly be any loose ends by the final stage. So it would seem. According to author Damon Chappie, that is not the reality. As he stated in *Roll Call Online*, "After a period of relative calm since Republicans took control of the House that may have been assisted by the overall weakening of the committee system and the centralization of power in leadership offices, chairmen are back to fighting about their committee jurisdiction."

"The latest squabble was sparked by a House Appropriations plan to turn a major tax program over to the military as well as by numerous other directives on tax policy."[9] Chairman Bill Archer (R-Texas) and other leaders of the Committee on Ways and Means, including those of the minority, in a letter addressed to Robert Livingston (R-Louisiana), Chairman of House Appropriations, strongly objected to the attempt to invade their jurisdiction. One can only imagine how long the process must be to work out the legalese that would end such jurisdictional disputes!

At any rate, even after all the above-mentioned steps, there still has been no permission given to any government agency to actually spend money. Only the program totals have been decided. The 13 cardinals and their subcommittee colleagues (but more importantly at this stage, their staffs) are next in leading the process.

Here is where the Appropriations Committee diverges most from other committees in the House. "Appropriators control the only legislation that must be approved every year. . . . While cardinals of the majority party dominate the allocation process, their subcommittees are perhaps the only institutions on Capitol Hill that maintain a tradition of bipartisanship."[10] There are several reasons for this relatively rare harmony.

According to Munson, the staff directors of subcommittees are "known by the purposely unassuming title of clerks." These top staff members are perhaps the only ones who entirely understand the appropriations process. Committee members have long recognized how important it is to retain their services.

The amount of government funding upon which Appropriations actually can make decisions is limited to discretionary funds, about one-third of the total. "Since the law enables a single lawmaker to block any spending above a subcommittee's allocation with a simple point of order . . . each cardinal uses every nickel allotted to him and then rejects virtually all amendments," Munson notes. "[T]he allocation of the federal budget among the thirteen Appropriation Subcommittees is the most closed, the least understood but the most consequential annual process within the Congress of the United States."[11] Most analysts of the appropriations process agree that the experienced, professional staff, which continues from Congress to Congress, makes most of the "multi-billion-dollar judgments" in the annual federal budget.

Although the two-step authorization-appropriation system is the norm, the full Appropriations committee can and does give federal agencies permission to spend funds on programs not yet authorized. Appropriations also need not spend entire amounts authorized by the concurrent resolution. In fact, if it chooses, it does not have to appropriate any funds for a program at all. What it cannot do is appropriate more money to a program than has been authorized in the concurrent resolution.

Should passage of the concurrent resolution be delayed overlong, House appropriators can still go ahead with their work. Constitutionally, the House must originate money bills. Therefore, the Senate Appropriations Committee usually awaits receipt of the House version of the bill before it begins its own deliberations.

Appropriation laws are vital for keeping the government running once a new fiscal year has begun. Permission can be given to federal agencies to continue operations at the same spending levels voted in the most recent budget. Measures containing this permission are called continuing resolutions. They have the force of law until finally changed by passage of a new budget. "Because so few money bills clear Congress by the deadline, the continuing resolution is essentially a budget. It is all but certain of presidential approval and is so massive that there is little chance to question any items placed on it by Appropriations Committee members."[12]

In late 1995, problems that shut down parts of the government arose from this stage in the process. Some of the bills passed by the Republican-controlled Congress were not acceptable to President Clinton, a Democrat who vetoed some of the resulting laws. Without appropriations giving them permission to continue, a number of federal agencies had to stop work until Congress and the president could resolve their differences. It is interesting to note that a large number of Republican freshmen had been appointed to the Appropriations subcommittees. This group was united in asking for many changes in a number of federal programs before agreeing to an extension of funding. Congress watchers have observed that junior members serving on Appropriations committees may be more powerful than other members who have served perhaps for decades but don't happen to be on those committees.

When the staffs of the Appropriations subcommittees settle down to divide up the discretionary funds for the next budget, they have two important gauges to assist them. One is the

A tourist peeks into the National Air and Space Museum in 1995. The museum, along with other federal buildings and agencies, closed after President Clinton vetoed certain appropriations bills passed by Congress. Without permission to continue their operations, some federal agencies had to shut down until Congress and the president agreed on new appropriations bills.

president's new set of proposals and the other is the new authorizations that have been completed by the legislative committees and, in particular, the Ways and Means Committee in the House. At this point, the chairpersons of the Appropriations subcommittees are feeling pressure from almost everyone with an interest in the government's spending: the federal agencies, lobbyists, the President, majority and minority leaders, other committee and subcommittee chairpersons, and the public.

One group involved remains calm. "The staff profession-als don't fear political threats of individual representatives, ig-nore lobbyists, trust few outsiders."[13] Much of their creativity today is expended on figuring ways to ascertain proper juris-dictions, curtail legislative committees' requests for overly ex-pensive programs, and keep their appropriations within budget limits set by law.

After the staff have finished their work, the chairperson and ranking minority member of the subcommittee review the suggestions. Next, the full committee meets and handles the bill as regular legislation. Earlier discussions between members of the federal agencies and staff of the Appropriations subcom-mittees have eliminated many potential sticking points. Budget officers of those agencies and staff members generally have a harmonious relationship. If formal hearings are conducted, they are normally for the purpose of information gathering. Issues are not the focus. Rather, "witnesses tend to concentrate on money matters rather than policy."[14]

Appropriations subcommittee chairpersons are now in their element. This is the time for doing favors and for paying off their own obligations to colleagues. At this stage, a good deal of the infamous "pork" is added to the requests made by the legislative committees. Money is even appropriated for projects without the knowledge of the agencies that will benefit. The shrinking budget has made serious cuts to this time-honored congressional activity, but no one is willing to foretell when, if ever, this particular game will end.

Another interesting budget technique practiced on the sidelines is emergency spending. In situations such as war, nat-ural disaster, or terrorist activities, budget constraints can be avoided by declaring that expenditures are in response to an emergency. Then, the committees need not worry that their budgets will be affected by excess spending. There will be no need to take funds from other programs to pay for these inci-dents.

One of the many methods Congress tries for reducing spending is called scoring. The Office of Management and Bud-get and the Congressional Budget Office keep "scorecards" of

funds spent on federal programs. The major categories are domestic, international, and defense, and appropriators are forbidden to "raid" one account to send funds to another. It requires a good deal of horse trading among committees to stay within the limits set on each.

When the 13 subcommittee bills are finally completed, they must be approved by the full committee. "Full committee markups are usually rubber-stamp events since appropriators rarely challenge their colleagues, believing the subcommittee with expertise knows best and fearing other appropriators might retaliate."[15]

Even though the House and Senate versions of appropriation bills may be close, there is little doubt that a conference committee will be needed to make them identical. The Senate Appropriations committee is divided into the same basic 13 subcommittees. Even so, the House bill has usually been amended a number of times in Senate subcommittees before it reaches the conference. "Professional staffers quietly dominate conference proceedings, and most hover near the cardinals, nodding their approval or rejection of written amendments from the other side, often without consulting the lawmakers."[16]

When the conference committee has made its decisions, the staff writes the final bill, the committee report, and explains the points covered in the measure. Staff in the Senate include a report on the disposition of any amendments they have made to the House bill. Munson observes, "Congressional rules require that the conference report be filed for at least three legislative days before the House and Senate can vote on the compromise measure."[17] Even when the budget bill becomes law, there is no time for a sigh of relief. All the people involved are already working on the next budget.

Chapter 6

A RECIPE FOR FAILURE: HUAC

*When members of Congress see a pressing interest
or political advantage to interjecting themselves
into the administrative side of government, they
can do so—in contrast to legislators in other
countries—with relative ease.*
—JOEL ABERBACH, *Keeping A Watchful Eye:
The Politics of Congressional Oversight* (1990)

Programs approved by Congress and created to carry out national policies are administered by the executive branch. Congressional committee responsibility, however, does not end with yearly authorizing and appropriating for the nation. There is still the actual spending to be done. Not all programs are subject to the annual budget process, which provides a periodic review. So keeping track of how executive branch agencies are performing their duties is another major responsibility of congressional committees.

Oversight does not always mean the same thing to everyone. In programs in which there have been no scandals and things are running well, a committee member can take credit for the successes. When there have been highly visible and controversial problems with government programs, however, constituents are not shy about blaming elected officials. Discontent with their representatives can surface at any time, but committee members know that at election time their prospects are certainly not improved by unhappy voters.

As the complexity of governing the United States increases, Congress must change the way it works. Revisions of the 1946 Legislative Reorganization Act, for example, encouraged the establishment of oversight subcommittees and called for additional staff for standing committees whose responsibilities included overseeing executive agencies. The revisions required congressional staff to conduct oversight studies and report the findings to the full chambers of both houses. "[C]learly the professional staff are the eyes and ears for the committee leadership in their relationships with the bureaucracy. If staff cannot do the job, the situation is often bleak."[1]

At the opening of Congress in 1995, there was an additional and notable change: the creation of the House Government Reform and Oversight Committee. Its mission is to "review and study, on a continuing basis, the operation of Government activities at all levels with a view to determining their economy and efficiency." Three committees were combined to form this new oversight entity. It is now the "chief investigative committee of the House, with the authority to conduct government-wide oversight."

According to information provided on the Internet, the committee "has two fundamental responsibilities: (1) it acts as the principal oversight committee of all Executive Branch agencies, programs, and activities, and (2) it exercises legislative jurisdiction over a diverse set of activities ranging from budget and procurement reform to reorganizations of the Executive Branch."

The Budget and Accounting Act of 1921 had already established the General Accounting Office (GAO), the main investigating arm of Congress. This is now the largest congressional oversight agency. The agency's chief officer, the Comptroller General, is appointed by the president with the advice and consent of the Senate. Currently, the GAO has more

Lobbyists, congressional staffers, and the press line the hall of Congress, awaiting a committee hearing.

than 4,500 employees and an annual budget exceeding $400 million. Responding to specific requests from congressional committees (and less frequently from individual members), the GAO "is charged with examining all matters relating to the receipt and disbursement of public funds."[2]

The executive branch has its own overseers, the Inspectors General. Created in 1978 by an act of Congress, there is now an Office of Inspector General in each of 61 federal agencies. Their mission includes conducting audits and investigations to detect or prevent fraud and waste in agency programs. Add to this congressional task forces, independent regulatory commissions, and the more than 1,000 advisory committees whose investigations include technical questions and legislative issues, and it begins to seem as if investigating is the most important game in town.

Checking to see if things are going wrong is not the only reason for oversight. Equally important to congressional committees is making sure things are going right. Professor Joel Aberbach explains in his book, *Keeping a Watchful Eye*, that "it is common for Congressional committees to develop a proprietary view of the programs in their jurisdictions," that "only the rare committee unit was willing to see the programs in its jurisdiction cut in favor of another unit's programs."[3] and that "most oversight takes place in a general advocacy context."[4]

As was noted earlier, members who seek specific assignments often do so because of a prior interest in a particular committee's jurisdiction. They also choose seats on committees that give them opportunities to benefit their constituents. As a major part of their efforts on Capitol Hill goes toward committee duties, overseeing federal programs they have helped create is a task they look forward to undertaking. Protecting those programs from jurisdictional wars and budget cutters requires that the members know how their favorite programs are faring. Oversight help comes from constituents, staff, lobbyists, special interest groups, and federal program managers, all of whom have a vested interest in seeing that favored programs are kept alive.

Congressional committees use many techniques in oversight: hearings, evaluations, audits, field studies, public opinion polls, and many formal and informal communications between congressional staffers and executive branch contacts. Professor Aberbach found "top staffers compensate in part for any training or experiential deficiencies by maintaining an extensive network of contact with relevant members of the executive branch."[5] Those questioned for the study indicated that these contacts are frequent, generally amiable, and provide a constant flow of information on program and agency activities.

Many members of Congress are better known for the some of the national programs they have helped create than for activities in their home states. In those cases, oversight is mostly important for helping the program or agency survive. Efficiency is not ignored, but cost-cutting is given a much lower priority. Seeing that the program survives is generally the member's fondest wish.

Choosing to perpetuate specific federal programs and agencies depends on a number of things, not the least of which is the member's overall philosophy. Occasionally the mood for cutting spending overcomes a committee's natural instinct to assure the survival of its favorite projects. For example, on July 14, 1996, two major newspapers carried stories that indicate results of current oversight attitudes in Congress. The *New York Times* reported that the GAO's program evaluation division is being dismantled,[6] and the *Washington Post* reported that the House Commerce Committee would like to privatize key functions of the Food and Drug Administration.[7]

The GAO is one of the programs created specifically for the use of congressional overseers. The Food and Drug Administration is a federal program with its own enthusiastic committee sponsors. These two programs are known to have strong support among members of both parties in Congress and with public advocacy groups. Budget constraints can and do require budget cuts such as these, but political philosophy determines where, how much, and when.

Unfortunately, oversight is not always benign and can be far from democratic. The history of the House Un-American Activities Committee illustrates how true this is. The lesson the nation learned was that giving such unlimited oversight power to congressional committees can lead to abuse of that power.

THE HOUSE UN-AMERICAN ACTIVITIES COMMITTEE

In the early 1930s Congress investigated a number of groups in the United States who were openly sympathetic to Hitler and his Nazi party in Germany. Everywhere the economic situation was bleak, and Congress was dealing with many problems it had not faced before. The nation's mood was one of suspicion, even of some of its allies.

In 1937, Rep. Samuel Dickstein (D-New York) "introduced a resolution in language that opened up spectacular new investigative vistas." His resolution requested permission to conduct investigations of any organizations "found operating in the United States for the purpose of diffusing within the United States of slanderous or libelous un-American propaganda of . . . subversive political prejudices"[8] There was a major problem within the resolution. Nobody, including Dickstein, was able to define "un-American."

That resolution did not pass, but it was not the first, nor would it prove to be the last, of its kind to reach that august body. A similar resolution, also defeated, was proposed that same day by Rep. Michael Dies (D-Texas). He also wanted investigations of "subversive" and "un-American" groups. Not surprisingly, the two men joined forces, and three months later their wish was granted by a majority vote in the House.

In his study *The Committee*, Walter Goodman quotes the House resolution:

Resolved, that the Speaker of the House of Representatives be, and he is hereby, authorized to appoint a special committee . . . for the purpose of conducting an investigation of (1) the extent, character, and object of un-American propaganda activities in the United States, (2) the diffusion within the United States of subversive and un-American propaganda that is instigated from foreign countries or of a domestic origin and attacks the principle of the form of government as guaranteed by the Constitution, and (3) all other questions in relation thereto that would aid Congress in any necessary remedial legislation.

The experience the country went through because of this legislation certainly is one reason it now would be recognized—

and probably rejected—as inviting an open-ended "fishing expedition."

With the passage of this resolution, the Dies Committee was born, and what a fishing expedition it started. Dies had become an ardent opponent of the New Deal, the economic program President Franklin Roosevelt developed in response to the depression of the early 1930s. Although he called himself a friend of labor, Dies believed that the Congress of Industrial Organizations (CIO), one of labor's most politically active groups, was destroying the country. Actually, the country was truly in pretty bad shape. Quieting labor unrest was Dies's professed object. In fact, it turned out that he and some of his colleagues harbored prejudices against many groups: labor unions, Nazis, Marxists, Zionists, Communists, pacifists, liberals, writers, blacks, Jews, educators, students, and immigrants—to name a few.

Committee tactics were brutal. It leaked names of individuals, companies, and organizations taken from sealed testimony. These names were inserted into the *Congressional Record*, along with insinuations that those named were known to be Nazi sympathizers, spies, or worse—agitators. More than a few of the names had been taken from testimony whose secrecy was protected by the laws of the United States. Witnesses were badgered, their testimony ridiculed, their intentions impugned.

It has been suggested that the behavior of Dies, Dickstein, and others would perhaps provide a good definition for "un-American." At the time, there were no laws forbidding a U.S. citizen from being any of those things so unpopular with the congressional investigators. That did not stop the Dies Committee from making many witnesses feel they were being charged with some unknown crime against the United States.

Arrogance and the use of guilt by association became permanent standards for the investigations that followed the establishment of the committee. Some charged that its tactics were unconstitutional, but the special committee had loyal supporters and lived on. Not only did it live on, but in 1945 a permanent committee replaced the special committee, and the House Un-American Activities Committee (HUAC) came into being.

Next to feel the wrath of the investigators were government workers and movie stars. Under the chairmanship of Rep. J. Parnell Thomas (D-New Jersey), the ruthlessness continued. So brutal did the interrogations become that witnesses began invoking their Constitutional rights under the First Amendment (protecting free speech) and the Fifth Amendment (granting protection against self-incrimination). Prison and blacklisting followed, and people were thrown out of work. Several suicides were attributed to the unfairness of the committee's interrogators.

At times, the committee generated contempt of Congress citations that were too numerous even to be processed. Walter Goodman notes in *The Committee*, "During the Hiss hearings, Thomas . . . attempted to coerce a lawyer for one of the witnesses to give testimony regarding his advice to his client. When the lawyer refused to be sworn, Thomas lit into him. 'The rights you have are the rights given you by this Committee. We will determine what rights you have and what rights you have not got before this Committee.'"[9]

In its 28 years of life, HUAC (hue-ack) existed under seven presidents. Three of them would be closely involved with the committee.

Richard M. Nixon served on HUAC as a freshman in Congress in 1947. The future president was a primary Congressional investigator in the famous espionage trial of former State Department official Alger Hiss. Hiss had been accused of having been a Communist before the war. He was not found guilty of espionage, but HUAC tried him on perjury, and he was sent to jail.

Ronald Reagan, who would be elected president in 1980, was a movie actor during the early years of HUAC. Along with many others, he was questioned about subversive activities in the film industry. There were successive hunts for subversives in Hollywood. Although most of those accused were among the writers and producers, Washington was visited by wave after wave of movie stars who came to testify for and against members of their industry.

The committee, amid all the media extravaganzas created

Hollywood studio chief Jack Warner testifies before the House Un-American Activities Committee in 1947. Studio heads, movie stars, and government officials were among the many people who testified before the committee, which sought to investigate so-called "un-American" organizations.

by the appearances of Hollywood stars, insisted it was getting advice to help decide if it should write legislation to outlaw Communism. If the stakes had not been so high, it would have been more like a circus than an investigation.

The third president to be directly involved had trouble with HUAC while he was in office. Harry S Truman became president upon the death of Franklin Roosevelt in 1945. Soon, Congress passed the Internal Security Act, a continuation of business as usual in the "seeking out" and investigating of subversives. Truman warned he would veto the Act. Congress passed it anyway.

Seeking out was one of the most repressive parts of the act. Truman had already agreed that government employees must take loyalty oaths. The Internal Security Act would have extended this to many other groups. When he vetoed it, Truman had evidently drawn the line at its mandate for registration and fingerprinting all "suspected subversives," plus the proposed establishment of concentration camps for certain types of "emergencies." He is reported to have thought the committee was probably the most un-American thing in America.

The Senate, while agreeing with the House in approving the "un-American" legislation, did not have the same investigative structure. The Committee on Government Operations (now Government Administration) set up a permanent Subcommittee on Investigations, and in 1953, Senator Joseph McCarthy (R-Wisconsin) became its chairman. Illegal wiretaps, one-sided interrogations, blacklists, indictments, unsubstantiated accusations, all were used to seek out subversion.

Among the groups that had been harassed by the Dies Committee, HUAC, and the McCarthy investigations, including the State Department and the U.S. Army, very limited subversive activity was uncovered. One result of all this activity was that anyone who was a member of the Communist Party had to register with the government. Subversion or belonging to any group whose purpose was to overthrow the U.S. government was, and continues to be, against the law.

The Senate, to its credit, censured McCarthy for, among other things, his behavior during the televised hearings. The senator had assigned himself the starring role. *McCarthyism* is a word that has immortalized his ungentlemanly bullying and his abusive language. *Un-American*, however, still awaits a definition.

Congressional committee members are seldom censured. Even less frequently does either chamber let go of one of its committees. For example, the Committee of Revolutionary Claims was not abolished until 1921.[10] Fortunately, it did not take quite as long to abolish the House Un-American Activities Committee. In 1969 it was given a new name, the Internal Security Committee. Despite warnings by many groups and individuals that the committee habitually violated citizens' constitutional rights, its demise did not come about until 1975. As for McCarthy's committee, the Permanent Subcommittee on Investigations still exists but is now under the chairmanship of the highly respected William J. Roth, Jr., the senior senator from the state of Delaware. If the nation has learned its lesson, there will never be another attempt to define *un-American*.

Chapter 7

A RECIPE FOR SUCCESS: THE ENDANGERED SPECIES ACT

Over increasingly large areas of the United States, spring now comes unheralded by the return of the birds, and the early mornings are strangely silent where once they were filled with the beauty of bird song.
—RACHEL L. CARSON, *Silent Spring* (1962)

The U.S. Capitol sits on the top of a hill, dominating Washington from the highest spot in the nation's capital. No building in the District of Columbia is permitted to be taller than the majestic Capitol, on whose soaring dome stands the statue called Freedom. Less distinguished perhaps, but nonetheless extremely important, are the six buildings located to the right and left of the home of the U.S. Congress.

These block-long structures, three on each side of the magnificent Capitol, are the House and Senate office buildings. Connected to it by beautiful tree-lined pathways aboveground and subway tunnels below, these buildings represent the two sides of the Hill.

The U.S. Senate Russell Office Building is one of the six House and Senate office buildings.

The Hart Building, on the Senate side of the Hill, is the newest of the six. Nothing about the building's bland exterior hints at its airy, modern, wide-open center court surrounded by glass-walled interior corridors. Inside Room #407 of the Hart Senate Office Building, the Documents Room of the Senate Committee on Environment and Public Works, the atmosphere is completely different. Every wall, floor to ceiling, is lined with cabinets filled from top to bottom with government documents. There is barely enough room for the desks of the professional staff.

Amid the tons of paper in the Documents Room are thousands of pages that concern one of Congress's most awesome responsibilities: the protection of endangered species of plants and animals. Few matters commanding the attention of committee members generate more attention, from the public and special-interests groups alike, than does this vital and divisive issue.

Endangered species are not a new concern for the U.S. Congress. Declining numbers of domestic fish led Congress to establish the U.S. Fish Commission in 1871. Twenty years later, new legislation gave the executive branch power to protect large tracts of forest land from over-cutting. During his time in office (1901–9), President Theodore Roosevelt increased the lands already set aside by an additional 150 million acres. As early as 1940, Congress had noted the alarming decline of the nation's symbol itself, the bald eagle, and passed the Bald Eagle Protection Act. Ironically, the eagle had been used as a symbol of the country since 1782, longer than Congress had officially existed.

Early descriptions of this continent suggest there must have been many thousands of bald eagles, a bird that was then known to exist only in North America. By the early 1960s, the bald eagle population had dropped to about 450 breeding pairs.

The publication of *Silent Spring* in 1962 marked a turning point in the history of concern over the environment. The author, Rachel Carson, was a respected scientist who had worked for the U.S. Fish and Wildlife Service for 17 years. During that time, Carson became aware of studies that described the harmful effects of pesticides then being used extensively on crop lands and forests. Especially dangerous to birds was DDT. Excerpts from her forthcoming book in *The New Yorker* magazine shocked its readers. The eventual publication of her book later that year is probably the single most important event in the now-extensive environmental protection movement. Ten years later, the use of DDT was banned.

Congress has passed a series of laws to guide the work of protecting plants and animals in danger of extinction. The most comprehensive of these is the Endangered Species Act of 1973. Although amended a number of times, this is still the main legislation concerned with the disappearance of plant and animal species.

The first official endangered species list was drawn up in 1967 for legislation that was a prelude to the Endangered Species Act. The nation's symbol, the bald eagle, was on it. The original list had 78 species; it now contains more than 800 and about 50 are added each year. On a happier note, in July 1995, the bald eagle was removed from the endangered species list and placed on the threatened species list, meaning its numbers and range had increased.

According to Section 3 of the Endangered Species Act of 1973, endangered species means any species that is in danger of extinction throughout all or a significant portion of its range. Threatened species means any species that is likely to become an endangered species within the foreseeable future throughout all or a significant portion of its range.[1]

Senate jurisdiction for this crucial responsibility has been assigned to the Subcommittee on Drinking Water, Fisheries, and Wildlife. To say the least, it is a very busy committee. Just one document compiling testimony from only three days of hearings runs to almost 1,500 pages. Those pages were accumulated from testifiers in only three states, Oregon, Idaho, and Wyoming.

A small sampling of any of the voluminous documents outlines the major concerns. For many, it is a question of economics—growth versus preservation. Others feel that Congress is not doing enough. The government itself comes in for some heavy criticism, as it owns millions of acres that serve as habitat for many species in question.

Witnesses before the subcommittee have ranged from the American Farm Bureau to Zip-o-log Mills, Inc., a small sawmill owned by a family in Eugene, Oregon. Some of the points brought out in testimony from these and other witnesses are the following:

Different protections should be afforded species that are listed as "threatened" than for those listed as "endangered." Protections and prohibitions applicable to

The bald eagle was on the first official endangered species list. The Senate Subcommittee on Drinking Water, Fisheries, and Wildlife is responsible for overseeing the regulations under the Endangered Species Act.

threatened species should be published on a case-by-case basis as part of the final listing rule.

—CARL LOOP, VICE PRESIDENT,
AMERICAN FARM BUREAU FEDERATION

As presently written, the Act is so profoundly unfair to landowners because it shifts the burden of protecting listed species and their habitat away from the federal agencies and onto private landowners.

—STEVEN P. QUARLES, COUNSEL,
AMERICAN FOREST & PAPER ASSN.

Owners and potential buyers may not know whether particular properties plays [*sic*] host to endangered species. Observers report that bureaucratic judgments appear to be inconsistent from one property to another.

—CHARLES E. GILLILAND, PH.D.,
REAL ESTATE CENTER AT TEXAS A & M UNIV.

The death of the owner of the tract has placed its future in doubt. The tract has been valued by the Internal Revenue Service according to its development potential. The resulting estate tax liability has forced the heirs to consider liquidating most of the land's timber assets, thereby destroying most of its ecological significance.

—MICHAEL J. BEAN, ENVIRONMENTAL DEFENSE FUND

Section 7(A) of the ESA requires each federal agency, in consultation with the U.S. Fish and Wildlife Service or the National Marine Fisheries Service, to insure that its actions are not likely to jeopardize the continued existence of any threatened or endangered species or result in the adverse modification of a listed species' critical habitat. Currently, litigation brought under ESA is moving federal land management away from federal agencies and into the federal courthouse.

—MIKE WHITE, VICE PRESIDENT AND
GENERAL COUNSEL OF HECLA MINING CO.

84

Other topics that should be addressed by Congress under re-authorization include: the need to improve the scientific base for listing, recovery, and de-listing decisions by requiring the use of all applicable scientific data and the application of rigorous scientific standards to the data used; by requiring additional research be undertaken when existing data are inadequate; and by requiring outside peer review as a standard part of the process in developing reports, drawing conclusions, and reaching decisions.

—Dr. James Sweeney, Manager,
Wildlife Issues, Champion International Corp.

Cattlemen are justifiably apprehensive to acknowledge that they have endangered species on their property because of the potential punitive penalties, stiff fines, lawsuits, and land use restrictions and loss of land values that have resulted from the law. In the southwest, for example, ranchers who used to help the desert tortoise are very wary to even go near the animal, now that they are federally listed.

—Jimme L. Wilson, President,
National Cattlemen's Assn.

At the opening of hearings on March 2, 1995, Senator Dirk Kempthorne (R-Idaho) stated: "As the new chairman of the Senate subcommittee responsible for the Endangered Species Act, I want to ensure that this committee, as we deal with that issue in its entirety, will thoughtfully and thoroughly review the law, its regulations, and court interpretations. . . . This Act on its present course of heavy regulation and putting people and communities at risk won't work." Later, Kempthorne mentioned in his opening remarks at the June 1, 1995, field hearings on reauthorization of the Endangered Species Act: "The fact that hundreds of you are here makes it very clear to all of us that the Endangered Species Act has significant impact for you. As I'm sure we'll hear today, that im-

Senator Dirk Kempthorne appears at a January 1995 press conference. Kempthorne is the chairman of the Senate Subcommittee on Drinking Water, Fisheries, and Wildlife.

pact may be positive and it may be negative, but every one of you here feels strongly or you wouldn't be here to advocate either its continuation unchanged, modification or its outright elimination."

Meanwhile, the House Endangered Species Act Task Force, chaired by Rep. Richard Pombo (R-California), also held field hearings in 1995. According to Pombo's office, more than 8,000 people attended the field hearings. Suggestions from those hearings echoed those of the Senate: improve the scientific methodology for identifying endangered species, extend the process to more people, include economic incentives, and use regional approaches to the problems.

Members of the Black Bear Conservation Committee, "a coalition of landowners, state and federal agencies, private conservation groups, forest industries, agricultural interests, and the academic community," may have the most important idea of all: cooperation among the individuals and groups with a stake in the survival of species. According to the Black Bear Conservation Committee's spokesperson, Murray Lloyd, "we chose instead to form a group with representation from all stake holders who agreed to leave their organizational biases at the door and work together to identify the most expansive common ground that was least intrusive on private landowners."[2]

The nine-member Senate subcommittee has an enormous job. It must cover a very wide range of issues when dealing with endangered species. That range is not limited to the United States, but actually extends all around the world. Countries having any trade with the United States must be aware of the laws. The United States has more than 40 treaties with, among others, Native American nations, Japan, Canada, Mexico, and Russia.

It is difficult to exclude any segment of the government from the subcommittee's purview, but at the very least involved in its oversight responsibilities are programs in the U.S. departments of the Interior, Commerce, Agriculture, and Justice, plus a number of programs within independent agencies, such as the Environmental Protection Agency. Even the Department of Defense has been involved as hearings were held regarding the endangered species in and around Fort Bragg, North Carolina.

When the environmental movement was at its height, there seemed to be three distinct groups whose interests were at odds: the environmental lobby, economic interests, and the federal government. Happily, that is no longer the case. All parties seem to be calling for cooperation and attention to the seriousness of the problem and changes needed in the legislation. Vital interests are surfacing for everyone with a stake in preservation of plant and animal life. That would mean all of us.

Chapter 8

CONGRESSIONAL COMMITTEES: BUILDING AND CHANGING THEIR OWN WORLD

There can be no progress if people have no faith in tomorrow.
—John F. Kennedy, Nov. 18, 1963

The surest thing that can be said about congressional committees is that they will change. New leaders will face new problems and will try to resolve them within committees. Because of the fundamental differences between the committees of the House of Representatives and of the Senate, arriving at the solutions to these problems will be a little more difficult to find.

Although Congress has operated for more than 200 years, "the history of selecting leaders does not go back nearly so far as 1798; the process and every office except Speaker, which was created in the Constitution, evolved only in [the twentieth] century."[1] The position of Speaker of the House, then, is one of the major differences between the two chambers.

Prompted by its Constitutional prerogative for a strong, centralized leadership, the House is run under much stricter rules than the Senate, and majority power is exercised in quite a different manner. Each committee is headed by a member of the majority party, and in the House this individual tends to be a loyal follower of the Speaker. Senate committee chairs, too, are of the majority party, but the behavior within committees reflects the difference in traditions that have developed over the last century.

Traditionally, the Senate has been inclined toward consensus building and bipartisanship, while the House tends to strongly reflect the ideology of the party represented by a majority of its members. Senators have been noted for the deference with which they treat one another. A lasting tradition of unanimous consent guides not only behavior on the floor of the Senate, but in committees as well. Although this tradition may be weakening, it is still the norm. The House has historically been the scene of more than one furious brawl among its members.

Reflecting their limited numbers, senators must serve on more committees and subcommittees than their counterparts in the House. Consequently, members of the House tend to be more expert on the issues covered by the one or two committees on which they serve. Because of their fewer numbers and far larger constituencies, senators are more dependent upon their professional staff at all times. House members are not even permitted to have staff on the floor while debates are in progress.

The unique position of a strong Speaker of the House creates a style of leadership that affects committee behavior in several additional ways. Committee chairpersons confer in leadership meetings frequently. Although there are leadership meetings in the Senate, a good deal of communication goes on among minority and majority committee members, in informal settings as well as in scheduled committee meetings. Their staff are in constant communication with each other and with a wide spectrum of government and private interests.

To avoid time-consuming filibusters and the rarely successful cloture vote, committee leaders in the Senate are especially attentive to the concerns of their minority members prior to floor debates. Bill-killing amendments are not numerous, but other types are.

On the House side, though, "If a House committee has duly reported out a bill and its structure and substance have been approved by the Rules Committee, (a stop that Senate bills do not have to make), there is a strong resistance to any amendment offered on the floor, particularly if it comes from someone who is not a member of the bill-writing committee."[2]

In the Senate, failure to recognize a member during debate on a bill reported out by a committee is considered very bad form. In fact, a senator seeking recognition may be intending to introduce an entirely different bill to be tacked onto the one being considered. House members do not have this privilege. A greater percentage of the time-consuming bill writing during committee action never sees the light of day.

Observers have noted that senators get to know each other and form closer friendships with their colleagues more often than House members do. This includes friendships between members of opposite parties. In the 104th Congress, Speaker Newt Gingrich (R-Georgia) and House Minority Leader Richard Gephardt (D-Missouri), "have not had any official meetings or phone conversations in more than a year." This apparently "has led to a total breakdown in communication between the two leaders."[3] This situation is a bit more extreme than usual, even though House members have long been known to accuse the Senate of having a country club atmosphere. Service on more committees and fewer peers to get to know are two reasons given for the general amity in the Senate.

The placing of secret holds, the senatorial privilege that is not permitted in the House, may be coming to an end. Senate Majority Leader Trent Lott has responded to a bipartisan suggestion from two senators, Roy Wyden (D-Oregon) and Charles

Representative Richard Gephardt speaks to the press. The House Minority Leader was at odds with Speaker of the House Newt Gingrich during the 104th Congress.

E. Grassley (R-Iowa), that a study be made of some of the Senate's long-standing traditions.

The two senators have said they plan to begin making public announcements of holds in the *Congressional Record*. Lott has said, "Now I don't want to alarm anybody. I'm not advocating any massive changes. . . . I'm not committed to it yet, but I'm giving some thought to have a carefully selected, equally divided task force just to take a look at it, see if they've got any recommendations."[4] Another time-honored practice in the Senate is to avoid jumping into changes too quickly.

The power of seniority (not age, but office tenure), an almost sacred tradition in both houses, began to give way to committee leadership elections in the 1970s. For some time, when committee chairs were the most powerful members in both houses, the party leadership could almost be ignored. Then subcommittees sought and obtained more power in the 1980s, and full committee chairs lost a good deal of their clout. Later, limited budget funds handed a preponderance of power to all members of committees involved in the budget process, including but not limited to the chairpersons.

Although seniority is still used in committee assignments, it has fallen on much harder times in the House. Consider the chairmen of two of the three most important House Committees today: Appropriations and Budget.

As the 1996 edition of *The Almanac of American Politics* says of Rep. Robert Livingston (R-Louisiana):

Livingston's rise to the chairmanship of Appropriations was rapid and unexpected. He started the 103rd Congress as the fifth ranking Republican on the committee. . . . He had played little role in setting overall appropriations. Then the Republicans won control of the House and Senate and Speaker-to-be New Gingrich wanted a sympathetic chairman, willing to eliminate federal programs by giving them zero appropriations and sticking to it in conference.

Rep. John Kasich (R-Ohio) was elected to Congress in only 1982, yet a mere ten years later, he was chairman of the House Budget Committee. Both of these circumstances resulted from the end of a 40-year Democrat rule of the House and the strongly conservative attitudes of the new leadership.

Livingston has been put on notice by his party's leadership that the cardinals may be facing some heavy weather in the near future. He was given until December 1, 1996, to come up with suggestions for reorganizing the appropriations process. This request was puzzling only if one overlooks the highly controversial nature of the decision-making that must be done in the 13 subcommittees.

As pointed out by Damon Chappie in 1996, "The 131-year-old committee also has its own traditions and customs; the staff who work on it are considered to be the most thoroughly professional and prestigious in Congress." Livingston has told reporters, "I can't tell you at this point if we'll end up with fewer than the 13 subcommittees."[5] He expressed understandable concern about the possibility that the matching 13 subcommittees in the Senate might not make similar changes.

When Mary L. McNeil was researching for the publication of "How Congress Works," she found that party leadership in Congress was so divided among House Speaker, floor leaders, and committee chairpersons, that party discipline was impossible. As recently as the first session of the 104th Congress, it seemed likely that had changed. There were more than 70 freshmen in the House, and both houses were controlled by the same party. The anticipated party unity, however, has proved to be fickle. Although party unity is no longer as assured as was first believed, partisanship is alive and well. An extremely serious situation seems to be developing in Congress due to a rise in partisanship: the paralysis of conference committees.

Facing such sensitive issues as health care and welfare reform, Congress is finding itself dangerously close to a total breakdown in passing serious legislation. Committees of the two chambers are not being appointed in order to develop single bills from the separate House and Senate versions. "The House-Senate conference, an institution long used to resolve differences in legislation passed by both chambers, is falling into disrepair in the 104th Congress."[6]

As a result, several very important bills, approved by large majorities in both houses, have not reached the president's desk for signature. Both sides are passing the blame. One suggestion for the failure is that newer members don't realize the importance of the procedure. It is essential that both parties in both houses form a conference committee to work together, but reports are that even staffers are negotiating among themselves.

Conference committee action was considered to be one of the Congress's finer achievements because it provided an opportunity for exhibiting true leadership. The "College of Cardinals" is known to have been enthusiastic about the annual conferences with its Senate colleagues. Speaker Gingrich, through Livingston and the appropriations committee, may insist on a much closer leadership role, but it is difficult to imagine what process can effectively replace the conference committee's vital role in the budgeting process.

Usually the conference committee is a staple of congressional activity during the last few months before the fiscal year ends. (The Congress recesses for the month of August to campaign. In a presidential election year, this tradition is even more likely because the two political conventions are held in August.) Election year politics will always slow things down, but according to Adam Clymer of the *New York Times*, "The Senate, embroiled in a Presidential campaign as never before, may be surpassing itself in ineffectiveness."[7]

On the other hand, something more fundamental may be involved. Columnist Sidney Blumenthal points out that, "the 104th turns out to have been the least productive first-year Congress in modern American history. It enacted eighty-eight public bills. The first session of the 103rd Congress, by comparison, enacted two hundred and eleven—a figure on the low side of average."[8]

A large part of the problem was, of course, that the House leadership had just been changed, and the Senate faced a number of changes in leadership when majority leader Robert Dole (R-Kansas) resigned to run for president. Leadership changes in either house mean memberships are less cohesive, work is slowed, and committee members are moved around. It is likely the experiences of this particular Congress will weigh heavily in the controversial term limits movement. "In 1992 a combination of voluntary retirements and electoral defeats brought 14 new senators and 110 new representatives—the highest turnover since 1948."[9] "As the 103rd Congress settled in, 68

The 104th Congress meets in full session in February 1996. The 104th faced many internal problems, including legislative inexperience and partisan stalemate, as well as such difficult issues as welfare reform.

percent of representatives and 48 percent of senators had been elected to their posts during the preceding decade. The natural process of membership renewal, in other words, has not halted."[10]

Another extremely controversial issue is that of campaign finance reform. The grueling two-year cycle for each representative is now considered only moderately less difficult than the six-year senatorial cycle. Suggestions run from financing campaigns entirely from public funds to taking all limits off certain sources of contributions.

The Capitol has been the legislative center of the United States since 1800. In 1996, voters returned Republican majorities to both chambers of Congress.

Committees are not unaffected by this question. Recently, "[t]wo House members entangled in races for powerful committee posts have been donating their campaign money to other members, in a move that some colleagues believe is intended to bolster their support for these positions."[11] A number of members have what are considered safe seats, i.e., they will have no trouble being reelected. Achieving their desired committee posts, however, depends upon the votes of their peers. So, if there is money left over in their campaign accounts, those funds can be donated to their colleagues who can then help them obtain committee posts.

Considering that Congress has just narrowly escaped passing campaign finance reform legislation, and that House freshmen "received more than $24 million in campaign contributions in 1995," this sort of "horse-trading" does not appear to be in danger of disappearing. The public faces the age-old predicament: only Congress can change Congress. Will the next changes make things any better? Well, maybe yes, maybe no.

1996 ELECTION UPDATE

In the national elections of November 1996, fewer than 50 percent of Americans who have registered went to their polling places to vote. Consequently, the 105th Congress was selected by the lowest percentage of eligible voters in 72 years. Voters reelected a Democratic president and returned Republican majorities to both houses of Congress—rare occurrences in recent elections.

On the whole, the profile of the new Congress is much like that of the 104th: majority and minority numbers vary only slightly; committee structures remain basically the same; top leadership is largely unchanged in both the House and the Senate.

A few important differences do exist between the two. There are subtle but notable shifts in power: some institutional, some personal. The public made no secret of its disapproval of Congress for government shutdowns, for its paltry record on legislation, and for its bouts of excessive partisanship. Surveys indicated the public tended to place much of the blame upon the Republican leadership in the House.

The electorate's displeasure was evident by the early summer of 1996. Subsequently, the cardinals (chairmen of the 13 House Appropriations subcommittees) and President Clinton wasted no time in reaching agreement on the next annual budget. The budget bill was completed, passed without fanfare in both houses, and signed by the president—all before the end of the fiscal year on September 30.

Between the election and the start of the new session in January, very little national business is carried on by Congress. Essential committee activity does continue, but newly elected members have their hands full just learning their duties and finding their way around Capitol Hill. After the campaign, a third of the senators and those representatives returning to the House begin the biennial round of moving offices, meeting their new colleagues, briefing and being briefed by staff.

Immediately after a general election, members face the start of yet another campaign: lobbying colleagues and obtaining endorsements for committee posts they want in the new session. In both houses, changes made in the 104th Congress appear to be having some unintended consequences. Seniority is still honored in the Senate, but it no longer guarantees there will be no surprises in committee assignments. As Jennifer Senior pointed out in *The Hill* on November 13, 1996, "In order to diffuse the effects of seniority and empower its newer members, the Senate Republican conference redrafted its rules . . . so that no chairman of any standing committee, with the exception of Rules and Appropriations, could also chair a subcommittee." In this Congress, as a consequence, some subcommittees will be chaired by newer members and others may be disbanded for lack of leaders willing or experienced enough to head them.

Things are even a little messier in the House of Representatives. For example, one of the changes in House rules made at the start of the 104th Congress has created a serious problem for the 105th. As the *Washington Post* reported in a column by John E. Yang on November 22, 1996:

House Majority Leader Richard K. Armey (R-Texas) called yesterday for a bipartisan agreement on whether the makeup of the House ethics committee should change—a politically charged issue because of the committee's continuing investigation into House Speaker Newt Gingrich (R-Ga.). . . . The question arises because when the current Congress goes out of existence in January, seven of the 10 committee members will have served three terms—the maximum length of service that House rules allow.

Such investigations are conducted by a four-member subcommittee. The findings remain confidential until a report is sent to the full committee. Therefore, the investigation would have to be started all over again by a reconstituted subcommittee. It would appear that neither Republicans nor Democrats favor that solution to the problem. Currently, the Clinton administration and members of both Congressional bodies are calling for working together in harmony. Resolving this case will provide a revealing test of their sincerity.

SOURCE NOTES

INTRODUCTION

1. Steven S. Smith and Christopher J. Deering, *Committees in Congress* (Washington, D.C.: Congressional Quarterly, 1990), p. xi.

2. George B. Galloway, *History of the House of Representatives*, rev. ed. edited by Sidney Wise (New York: Crowell, 1976), p. 9.

3. Ibid., pp. 46–47.

4. "The Senate Hears a Word from Byrd on a Manner of Speaking," *Washington Post*, Dec. 21, 1995. For a different perspective, see "Trench Warfare in Congress," *The Hill*, May 8, 1996.

CHAPTER 1

1. Roger H. Davidson and Walter J. Oleszek., *Congress and Its Members*, 4th ed. (Washington, D.C.: Congressional Quarterly, 1996), p. 203.

2. Smith and Deering, p. 2.

3. Mary L. McNeil, ed., *How Congress Works* (Washington, D.C.: Congressional Quarterly, 1983), p 41.

4. Smith and Deering, p. 8.

5. Helen Dewar, "Senate Kills Campaign Finance Bill," *Washington Post.* June 26, 1996, p. 4A.

6. Smith and Deering, p. 22.

7. Tracy White, ed., *Power in Congress* (Washington, D.C.: Congressional Quarterly, 1987), p. 63.

8. McNeil, p. 47.

9. Ibid., p. 41.

10. "Duties of the Parliamentarian of the House of Representatives." Memorandum, Nov. 21, 1994.

11. Paul Dickson and Paul Clancy, *The Congress Dictionary: The Ways and Means of Capitol Hill* (New York: Wiley, 1993), pp. 245–46.

CHAPTER 2

1. Walter J. Oleszek, *Congressional Procedures and the Policy Process*, 4th ed. (Washington, D.C.: Congressional Quarterly, 1996), p. 100.

2. Garry Young and Joseph Cooper, "Multiple Referral and the Transformation of House Decision Making," in Lawrence C. Dodd and Bruce I. Oppenheimer, eds., *Congress Reconsidered*, 5th ed. (Washington, D.C.: Congressional Quarterly, 1993), p. 215.

3. Walter J. Oleszek, *Congressional Procedures and the Policy Process*, 3d ed. (Washington, D.C.: Congressional Quarterly, 1989), p. 102.

4. Martha Gelbart, "House GOP Weighs New Powers for GAO Aides," *The Hill*, May 8, 1996.

5. Smith and Deering, pp. 123–24.

6. Oleszek, 4th ed., p. 111.

7. Stanley I. Bach, "House Rules and Precedents Affecting Committee Markup Procedures," *CRS Report for Congress*, No. 95-253, Feb. 8, 1995.

8. Smith and Deering, p. 143.

9. Ross K. Baker, *House and Senate* (New York: Norton, 1989), p. 56.

10. Ibid., p. 46.

11. "Duties of the Parliamentarian of the House of Representatives," Memorandum, Nov. 21, 1994.

12. McNeil, p. 46.

13. Smith and Deering, p. 10.

14. McNeil, p. 62.

15. Smith and Deering, p.143.

CHAPTER 3

1. David S. Broder, "No Friends Among Foes," *Washington Post,* June 23, 1996. p. C7

2. Norman J. Ornstein, Robert L. Peabody, and David W. Rohde, "The U.S. Senate in an Era of Change," in Dodd and Oppenheimer, pp. 13–40.

3. Oleszek, 4th ed., p. 328.

4. Judith Bentley, *Speakers of the House* (New York: Franklin Watts, 1994), p. 17.

5. Oleszek, 4th ed., p. 131.

6. Smith and Deering. p. xi.

7. McNeil, p. 111.

8. Ornstein, Peabody, and Rohde, p. 20.

9. Dan Morgan, "House Leadership Bends to Backbenchers' Muscle," *Washington Post,* Oct. 13, 1995.

10. Dan Morgan, "Steep Learning Curve for Appropriators," *Washington Post*, Nov. 2, 1995.

CHAPTER 4
----

1. Guy Gugliotta, "Hill Officials Organize to Fight Proposed Rules Allowing Staffers to Form Unions," *Washington Post,* July 9, 1996. p. A13.

2. Helen Dewar, "Senate Kills Campaign Finance Bill," *Washington Post*, June 26, 1996, p. 4.

3. Ibid.

4. Adam Clymer, "Senate Kills Bill to Limit Spending in Congress Races," *New York Times,* June 26, 1996, p. A1.

CHAPTER 5
----

1. Davidson and Oleszek, p. 396.

2. White, p. 60.

3. Ellen Miller, "Gimme A (Tax) Break," *The Hill*, May 8, 1996, p. 32.

4. "Jurisdiction of the Committee on Ways and Means," Committee Print WMCP:103–29, 1994.

5. Ibid.

6. Oleszek, 4th ed., p. 143.

7. Ibid., p. 66.

8. James A. Thurber, "The Ups and Downs of the Appropriations Committee," *Roll Call Online*.

9. Damon Chappie, "Turf Wars Re-Ignite In House," *Roll Call Online*, July 9, 1996.

10. Richard Munson, *The Cardinals of Capitol Hill: The Men and Women Who Control Government Spending* (New York: Grove Press, 1993), p. 6.

11. Munson, pp. 11–12.

12. "Maintaining Order In the House," by Lawrence C. Dodd and Bruce I. Oppenheimer, *Congress Reconsidered,* p. 52.

13. Munson, p. 30.

14. Ibid., p. 13.

15. Ibid., p. 73

16. Ibid., p.178.

17. Ibid., p. 190.

CHAPTER 6

1. Joel D. Aberbach, *Keeping A Watchful Eye: The Politics of Congressional Oversight* (Washington D.C.: Brookings Institution, 1990), p. 81.

2. "About the U.S. General Accounting Office." GAO www Homepage. Excerpted from the U.S. Government Manual.

3. Aberbach, p. 33.

4. Ibid., p. 118.

5. Ibid., p. 83.

6. Tim Weiner, "Stealth, Lies and Videotape," *New York Times,* July 14, 1996, p. E3.

7. Morton Mintz, "The Cure That Could Kill You," *Washington Post,* July 14, 1996, p. C1.

8. Walter Goodman, *The Committee: the Extraordinary Career of the House Committee on Un-American Activities* (New York: Farrar, Straus and Giroux, 1968), pp.13–14.

9. Goodman, footnote p. 251.

10. McNeil, p. 94.

CHAPTER 7

1. *Endangered Species Act of 1973, As Amended Through the 100th Congress.* Serial No. 100-C. Washington, D.C.: GPO, 1988, pp. 3–4.

2. Testimony of Murray Lloyd before the Senate Committee

on Environment and Public Works Subcommittee on Drinking
Water, Fisheries and Wildlife, Aug 3, 1995.

CHAPTER 8

1. White, p. 5.
2. Baker, p. 76.
3. "Gingrich, Gephardt Endure Icy Standoff," *The Hill*, July 17, 1996.
4. Helen Dewar, "Lott Considers Task Force To Study System of Rules," *Washington Post,* July 18, 1996, p. A25.
5. Damon Chappie, "House GOP Plans to Launch Reform of Appropriations," *The Hill,* May 13, 1996.
6. Jamie Stiehm, "Hill Conferences Falling into Disuse," *The Hill*, July 17, 1996, p. 1.
7. Adam Clymer, "As Campaign Heats Up, Senate Just Stops Cold," *New York Times,* May 13, 1996, p. A12.
8. Sidney Blumenthal, "Our Next Prime Minister: Gingrich's Eclipse has Created a Dilemma for Dole," *The New Yorker,* May 20, 1996.
9. Guy Gugliotta, "Seniority—Soon It's Not in Kansas Anymore," *Washington Post*, June 4, 1996, p. A 15.
10. Davidson and Oleszek, pp. 114–15.
11. Craig Karmin, "Matsui, Oxley use Campaign Funds to Boost Committee Bids," *The Hill*, May 8, 1996. p. 3.

GLOSSARY

appropriation Legislation setting out amounts of money that can be spent by the federal government. The Constitution states that no funds from the U.S. Treasury can be spent unless approved by Congress and the president in the form of appropriations laws.

authorization Legislation that establishes new federal programs or gives federal agencies permission to continue already established programs. Limits on the total amount of money that can be spent on these programs are sometimes included. Instructions or guidelines for program managers are also included.

budget reconciliation Each year Congress must be certain the new budget does not conflict in any way with laws that have already been passed. Once the annual budget requests have been made, each legislative committee is asked to make sure there are no conflicts. If there are, these must be resolved through the legislative process.

calendar A listing of bills awaiting action in either the House or Senate. There are several varieties of calendars. The House has a total of five different ones. The Senate has one main calendar for legislative action and one for non-legislative action.

caucus A group whose members have identified themselves as sharing a special interest. In Congress, there are a number of such groups—including the Democratic Caucus, Republican Caucus, Women's Caucus, and Black Caucus—some of which have offices and staff to help achieve certain goals important to the membership.

cloture A special vote taken in the Senate to end a *filibuster*. It requires 60 votes under normal circumstances.

continuing resolution Temporary legislation authorizing the federal government to continue its operations until a new budget has been enacted. The procedure is required when the budget deadline of September 30 has not been met by the appropriations process.

filibuster A technique of continuous speech-making used by senators who wish to prevent certain bills from coming to the floor for debate. The Senate has devised a rule called *cloture*, which can be used to end the speeches.

fiscal year The federal government's annual calendar for operations. It runs from October 1 to September 30. Programs that have not been funded in the budget by September 30 must cease operations unless they are included in a continuing resolution passed by Congress and signed by the president.

germaneness How closely an amendment to a bill relates to the main points in the measure. House rules require that any amendment members want to make must be germane. Challenges to the germaneness of an amendment must be resolved before consideration continues. The Senate does not normally require that amendments be germane except during the consideration of appropriations bills.

hold A request by a senator that the majority leadership avoid bringing certain bills or nominations to the floor for debate. The leadership does not have to honor the request but can usually look for a *filibuster* should it refuse. Information about who has requested a hold is expected to be kept confidential.

mark up Final consideration of a bill by committee members and staff before the measure is sent for consideration by the full chamber

unanimous consent agreement A binding agreement worked out in advance of introduction of legislation on the Senate floor. Both majority and minority leaderships are involved in making the agreement. The details of the agreement will cover the way the measure will be handled during its consideration on the floor. Both houses have procedures for working out a unanimous consent to waive rules. This can be handled by voting procedures on the floor of either chamber.

SELECTED
BIBLIOGRAPHY

Aberbach, Joel D. *Keeping A Watchful Eye: The Politics of Congressional Oversight*. Washington, D.C.: Brookings Institution, 1990.

Baker, Ross K. *House and Senate*. New York: Norton, 1989.

Bentley, Judith. *Speakers of the House*. New York: Franklin Watts, 1994.

Committee on Rules and Administration, United States Senate. *Authority and Rules of Senate*.

Committees, 1995–96. Washington, D.C.: Government Printing Office, 1995.

Concurrent Resolution On the Budget-Fiscal Year 1997: Report of the Committee On the Budget: House of Representatives. House Report No. 104-575. Washington, D.C.: Government Printing Office, 1995.

Cwiklik, Robert. *House Rules*. New York: Ballard, 1991.

Davidson, Roger H. and Walter J. Oleszek. *Congress and Its Members*. 4th ed. Washington, D.C.: Congressional Quarterly, 1994.

Dickson, Paul. *The Congress Dictionary: The Ways and Meanings of Capitol Hill*. New York: Wiley, 1993.

Dodd, Lawrence C., and Bruce I. Oppenheimer. *Congress Reconsidered*. 5th ed. Washington, D.C.: Congressional Quarterly, 1993.

Drewry, Henry N., and Thomas N. O'Connor. *America Is*. New York: Macmillan/McGraw Hill, 1995.

Galloway, George B. *History of the House of Representatives*. New York: Crowell, 1976.

Goodman, Walter. *The Committee: The Extraordinary Career of the House Committee on UnAmerican Activities*. New York: Farrar, Straus and Giroux, 1968.

Harris, Fred R. *Deadlock or Decision: The U.S. Senate and the*

Rise of National Politics. New York: Oxford University Press, 1993.

McNeil, Mary L., ed. *How Congress Works*. Washington D.C.: Congressional Quarterly, 1983.

How Federal Laws Are Made: Citizens Guide to the Federal Law-Making Process. Washington, D.C.: Want, 1984.

Jackley, John L. *Hill Rat: Blowing the Lid Off Congress*. Washington, D.C.: Regnery Gateway, 1992.

Munson, Richard. *The Cardinals of Capitol Hill: The Men and Women Who Control Government Spending*. New York: Grove, 1992.

Oleszek, Walter J. *Congressional Procedures and the Policy Process*, Fourth ed. Washington, D.C.: Congressional Quarterly, 1996.

Penny, Timothy J., and Major Garrett. *Common Cents*. Boston: Little, Brown, 1995.

White, Tracy, ed. *Power In Congress: Who Has It, How They Got It, How They Use It*. Washington, D.C.: Congressional Quarterly, 1987.

Ripley, Randall B. *Party Leaders in the House of Representatives*. Washington, D.C.: Brookings Institution, 1967.

Smith, Steven S. and Christopher J. Deering. *Committees in Congress*. Washington, D.C.: Congressional Quarterly, 1990.

Taylor, Edward T. *A History of the Committee on Appropriations: House of Representatives*. Washington D.C.: Government Printing Office, 1941 [House Document No. 299].

Weatherford, J. McIver. *Tribes on the Hill*. New York: Rawson Wade, 1981.

Willett, Edward F. Jr. *How Our Laws Are Made*. Washington, D.C.: Government Printing Office, 1989 [House Document No. 101-39].

INDEX

Page numbers in *italics* indicate illustrations.

Livingston, Robert, 62, 92–94
Lobbyists, 39, 41, 44–46, 65, 66, *70*
Lott, Trent, 44, 90

McCain, John, 44, *45*
McCarthy, Joseph, 77–78
MacKay, Buddy, 49
Markup, 21–22, 25, 43, 47, 51, 67
Media, 41, 43, 47, *47, 70*
Medicare, *20,* 49, 55, 58
Memoranda of intent, 19
Mills, Wilbur D., 59
Multiple referrals, 18–19
Munson, Richard, 61, 63, 57

National Security Council, 11
Neumann, Mark W., 40
Nixon, Richard, 75

Office of Management and Budget, 51, 53, 66
Oversight, 56, 57, 68–72

Pombo, Richard, 86
President, U.S. *See* Executive office
President of the Senate. *See* Vice president

Rayburn, Sam, *35*
Reagan, Ronald, 75
Reconciliation, 54
Republican Committee on Committees, 33
Republican Policy Committee, 33

Republican Senatorial Campaign Committee, 33
Roosevelt, Franklin D., 32, 74, 77
Roosevelt, Theodore, 81
Roth, William J., 78

Scoring, 66–67
Select committees, 10–11
Select Committee on Presidential Campaign Activities (Watergate Committee), 10, *11*
Senate Appropriations Committee, 38, 62, 64, 67
Senate Armed Services Committee, 38
Senate Budget Committee, 52
Senate Committee on Environment and Public Works, 80–82
Subcommittee on Drinking, Fisheries and Wildlife, 82–87
Senate Committee on Government Administration, 77
Senate Committee on Government Operations, 77
Permanent Subcommittee on Investigations, 77–78
Senate Finance Committee, 38, 57
Senate Foreign Relations Committee, 38
Senate Office of Legislative Counsel, 16

111

Senate Parliamentarian, 17, 18, 19, 25
Senate Select Intelligence Committee, 11
Sequential referrals, 18, 19
Social Security, 49, *50,* 55, 58, 59
Speaker of the House, 13, 15, 17, 24, 25, *28,* 29, 30, 34–40, *35,* 44, 55, 61, 73, 88, 89, 93, 99
Special committees, 10–11
Split referrals, 18–19
Staff, 10, 40, 41–44, *42,* 45, 57, 61, 63, 64, 66, 67, 69, *70,* 89, 94
Standing committees, 10, 15–16, 54, 55, 69, 98

Subcommittees, 10, 16, 19, 20, 21, 34, 39–40, 43, 56, 57, 61, 62, 63–64, 65, 66, 67, 69, 77–78, 82–87, 92, 93, 94, 98, 99

Thomas, J. Parnell, 75
Truman, Harry S., 77

Unanimous consent, 24, 26, 27, 59

Vice president, 34, 36, 55

Whips, 33, 34
Wilson, Woodrow, 9, 41
Wyden, Roy, 90

DATE DUE

JAN 0 2 98			

The Library Store   #47-0102